How to Use the
Apple® II and IIe

How to Use the Apple ® II and IIe

Robert V. Price and Jerry Willis

dilithium Press
Beaverton, Oregon

10   9   8   7   6   5   4   3   2   1

Library of Congress Cataloging in Publication Data

Includes index.
1. Apple II (Computer) 2. Apple IIe (Computer) I. Willis, Jerry. II. Title.
QA76.8.A662P75 1984   001.64   84.1716
ISBN 0-88056-139-4

Cover: Eugene Gill

Printed in the United States of America

dilithium Press
8285 S.W. Nimbus
Suite 151
Beaverton, Oregon 97005

CONTENTS

Preface

This book was written for the Apple computer user who wants to learn quickly and conveniently the hows and whys of using the Apple IIe, the Apple II+, or the Apple II computer. Users of Apple "work-alike" computers — most notably the Franklin Ace and Orange Micro computers can also benefit from this book. Most of the information presented here is applicable equally to these work-alike computers.

This book is intended for the family, the teacher, the student, the hobbyist, or the business person who wants to make the best use of the Apple computer. It may serve as your first book on the Apple II computers, a primer that gets you started. It also can be useful as an introduction to practical applications of the Apple computer for any individual or group. We assume the reader has little prior experience with computing, but has a serious interest in getting the most from the Apple.

When you have finished this book, you should be able to comfortably operate your Apple, make informed decisions on selecting support products, establish your own computing priorities, and have a good basic knowledge of what the Apple computer can do.

Chapter 1

Introduction

USING THIS BOOK

This book covers the Apple IIe, the Apple II+, and the Apple II computers. These three members of the Apple family are very similar but have some important differences that will be pointed out carefully and explained. **Unless specifically stated otherwise, all information presented applies equally to the Apple II, II+, and IIe.**

In Chapter 1, the basics of getting started with the Apple are covered. Nothing is taken for granted. The basic Apple is described, and there's information on setting up the computer, using the keyboard, and a review is given of the modes in which the Apple can operate.

Loading and saving programs is covered in Chapter 2. There is a review of the text and graphics features of the Apple Computer. Some easy-to-use sample programs also are included.

Popular accessories such as disk drives, printers, monitors, clocks, RAM cards, and speech synthesizers are reviewed in Chapter 3. Specific products with producers and prices are included to help you decide which of these fit your needs.

In Chapter 4, maintenance — an often neglected area — is covered to help you keep your Apple up and running and to save you costly repair and "down time."

Programming in the BASIC language is covered in Chapters 5 and 6. After finishing these chapters, you should be able to write simple programs in Applesoft BASIC, create both low- and high-resolution graphics, and understand a program printed in a magazine or book.

In Chapter 7, you are given a review of all of the most important uses for your Apple. A procedure for selecting software is provided and popular programs are described to help you make decisions on which ones you need.

Chapter 8 provides information on where you can learn more. Which magazines should you subscribe to? Which books should you buy? Where can you buy support products, and which clubs and meetings should you attend?

An Index helps you locate specific topics.

One approach to using this book is simply to read it through from beginning to end. As you read, take time to try out the techniques presented and experiment with the Apple computer whenever you find something that strikes your fancy.

You may prefer to skip certain parts. For example, if you already are a proficient programmer or have little interest in programming, you may wish to skip Chapters 5 and 6. Each chapter is largely independent of the others and may therefore be read in any order desired. Chapters which are not of interest to you may be omitted.

A LITTLE FAMILY HISTORY

The newest version of the basic Apple is the Apple IIe. The earlier Apple II+ and Apple II, which are no longer in production, are essentially the same machines with a few important differences. The differences and their implications will be pointed out shortly. The Apple III, the Apple Lisa, and the MacIntosh are different computers entirely and will not be covered in this book.

Apple Computer has adopted a philosophy of continuing to support earlier models of its computers when new models are placed in production. Compatibility is an important concept with Apple. This means that newer Apples also can run most of the programs written for older Apples.

The Apple IIe was released in early 1983 and is a much improved version of the basic Apple II line. It still looks much like the older IIs and II+s. The main additional features are a better keyboard, fewer chips inside, an enhanced ability to display uppercase and lowercase letters, and an expanded rear input and output panel. The IIe uses the same Applesoft BASIC language and operating system as the II+. Most of the accessories and programs designed originally for the Apple II+ or II will work just fine on the IIe.

There are two primary differences between the Apple II and II+. The first of these is the version of the BASIC programming language supplied with the two machines. The original Apple II came with a version of BASIC called Integer BASIC. It was so labeled because this language is not capable of doing decimal arithmetic (although there are other limits as well). When the Apple II+ made its debut, an improved version of BASIC labeled Applesoft BASIC was included. The new version, developed for Apple by the Microsoft company, is a much expanded form of BASIC. It is sometimes referred to as "Floating-Point" or FP BASIC because it is capable of doing complex decimal arithmetic. The new FP, or Applesoft, BASIC is now available for the older IIs. Likewise, the earlier Integer BASIC can be easily added to the II+ so that programs written in this language can be run. (The Integer BASIC language is supplied on the "system master" disk which accompanies each Apple disk drive when it is purchased.)

The other major difference between the II and II+ is the "operating system." This is the program that controls the internal operations of the machine. The II+ is supplied with an improved operating system which is automatically activated when the computer is turned on. Either of the operating systems will operate with Integer or Applesoft BASIC.

The Macintosh is a transportable small computer which comes with 3½" disk drives and a built-in video monitor. This member of the Apple family was introduced in January 1984 and is designed for those who need a portable computer. The Mac's software may not be used on the Apple II's or III's but it may usually run on the Lisa.

The Apple III, in comparison to the Apple II line, is a more sophisticated, business-oriented machine. It has all of the capabilities of the II and II+, plus many others. The III will run most of the programs available for the IIs, but programs designed especially for the III are not directly transferable to the IIs. The Apple III is **not** intended as an updated version of the II or as a replacement for it.

The Lisa is even more sophisticated than the Apple III. It is so advanced that it is not directly compatible with any of the other Apples. The Lisa is a marvelous device intended for complex business applications. It is not an updated version of the IIs or the III. The Apple IIe, Apple III, Lisa , and Macintosh comprise the current product line for Apple Computer.

Your basic Apple is truly a marvelous and versatile little computer. More products, programs, and services are presently available for the Apple II, II+, and IIe than for any other small computer. Regardless of whether you are a business person, a hobbyist, or a teacher, you will find an abundance of uses for the Apple.

SET UP AND INSTALLATION

If you have just received your Apple or are just beginning to learn about it, a good starting point would be to review the main items which come

with the computer. The computer itself looks like a portable beige typewriter. If you have a disk drive unit, it is the rectangular box which will
sit on top of or beside the computer. Several cables may accompany the

FIGURE 1.1 The Apple IIe computer.

computer. One will be a video cable for connecting the computer to a TV
set or monitor. Disk drives have a short flat cable connected to them called
a ribbon cable. You also will need a TV or video monitor.

Your Basic Apple

To get some idea of how your Apple works, we'll take a look at its core
by removing the lid and checking out its insides. First, lift the lid on your
Apple straight up from the back with both hands and look inside.
The Apple IIe and II+ look quite different inside. The IIe has fewer
chips than the II+. You also will notice a red LED (light emitting diode)
at the left rear of the IIe circuit board. The IIe looks like this inside:

FIGURE 1.2 The Apple IIe motherboard.

A green circuit board called a "motherboard" can be seen inside the Apple. Numerous black rectangular chips are located on the motherboard. The largest of these is the microprocessor which has the number 6502 stamped on it. The 6502 chip is the heart of the Apple and processes all the information presented to your Apple computer by the programs you run.

If you look closely at the rows of smaller chips, you will notice some which are labeled ROM. These *read only memory* chips contain the BASIC programming language and the operating system. This information is permanently stored here, which means that you cannot delete or change it unless you program your Apple with a hammer. Several other rows of chips are labeled RAM. RAM stands for *random access memory*, and this is where your programs and data are stored while your Apple is in use. This area is wiped clean each time you turn off the computer or press

FIGURE 1.3 The Apple II+ motherboard.

the "reset" and the "control" keys together. At the back of the motherboard is a row of slots which are used to connect various devices such as printers and disk drives. The large "box" on the left side of the motherboard is the power supply. This provides the correct level of electrical current which the Apple needs to operate and filters out most electrical glitches and surges which can give computers fits.

On the right rear of the motherboard are several sockets for connection of various input and output devices. One is labeled "GAME I/O." This is where you connect your game controller paddles. The IIe also has a game I/O on the outside rear panel. Located near the game ports on the motherboard is a socket which is used to connect a "modulator." This is a device that lets you connect a standard TV to the computer.

FIGURE 1.4 The rear panel of the Apple IIe.

On the rear panel of the computer is the video output port where you may connect the Apple to a video monitor. Next to this are two jacks (or ports) labeled simply *in* and *out*. These are the ports used to connect your Apple with a cassette tape recorder.

Your basic Apple is of little value without a means of viewing the input to and output from the computer and a means of loading and saving programs. You will need a small television set or video monitor to use with

your Apple and either a cassette recorder or disk drive unit on which to
save your programs. You also may wish to connect a printer and game
controllers (or paddles) at this time.

Making the Connections

**As a safety precaution, turn off your Apple and unplug it before
making any connections.**

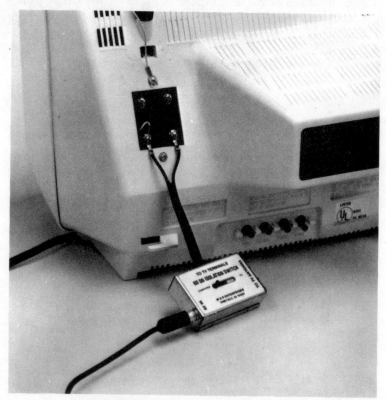

FIGURE 1.5 The T.V. monitor connections.

Connecting the TV. If you have either a monochrome or color monitor,
just plug it into the jack marked video on the back of the Apple with the
supplied video cable shown in the photo. (A black-and-white set will work
fine, but will not allow you to take advantage of the Apple's excellent
color graphics.)

If you are using a regular TV set, you will need an item called an RF modulator. This plugs into the port (output connection) inside the Apple which was shown and described previously. The port is located on the rear right area of the motherboard. The same cable used with a monitor also can be used to connect the modulator to the antenna leads on your television. Most modulators sold for use with the Apple connect to the VHF antenna leads on your TV rather than the UHF leads and will operate on a VHF frequency such as channel 3 or 4. (If there is a station in your area operating on the same or an adjacent channel to the one on which your modulator operates, your TV may receive both signals and produce a garbled mess on the screen. If you have a UHF modulator, you can sometimes correct this by tuning your TV to the UHF channel which is double its normal broadcast frequency (channel 66 in the case of a channel 33 modulator) and using this as your "computer channel." VHF modulators operate on channels 2-13 and are generally less subject to interference from other channels.

You will need a 300 ohm to 75 ohm adapter to connect the antenna leads on your TV. This usually comes with the modulator when you purchase it. Connecting the Apple to your TV does not impair its ability to receive regular TV stations. To watch television instead of communicating with the computer, simply move the slide on the 300-75 ohm adapter to TV and switch the channel selector to the desired channel.

FIGURE 1.6 The paddle connections on the Apple IIe.

FIGURE 1.7 Disk controller card placement.

The Game Controllers. Game controllers, or paddles, come in a variety of types, which will be discussed in Chapter 3. These plug into the game I/O ports described earlier. The IIe has an accessible game port on the rear panel to connect your controllers. Just connect them as shown in the photo. To connect game controllers to the II+, you must remove the cover and plug them directly into the port on the motherboard. The pins on the plug are very small and can be bent easily. When making this connection, be very careful to make sure that all the little pins go into the socket. Some game controller plugs are marked with a white or colored dot on one end. Make sure this goes toward the front or keyboard end of the computer.

The Disk Drive. A disk drive is the only reliable means of storing and saving your programs. Many programs are available only on disks. The only other common means of storing and saving programs which can be used with the Apple is a cassette tape recorder.

The disk drive will be connected via one of the slots (usually slot six) at the back of the motherboard through a controller card and a cable. First, connect the flat ribbon-like cable to the controller card. The controller card can be used with one or two disk drives. If you have only one disk drive, connect the cable to the set of pins labeled Drive 1. Be very careful here to make certain that the little pins on the controller card are aligned properly with the holes in the cable connection. If this is improperly connected, damage can result to the disk drive. The cable exits the connector **away from** the controller card. The other end of the cable should come firmly connected to the disk drive itself. If you are installing a second disk drive, it should be connected in the same manner to the set of pins labeled Drive 2.

To install the controller card, which you have connected to the disk drive via the ribbon cable, you simply plug the card into slot six, which is one place to the left of the right-most slot inside the Apple. Be certain to turn the power off before doing this! If the power is left on during removal or insertion of any card, serious damage can result to both the card and the computer. Insert the gold-colored fingers into the slot carefully. Some friction will be felt and the card should then seat firmly. Do not touch the gold fingers with your fingers. If you do, clean them with a soft cloth and alcohol before installing the card. Be sure the card seats evenly. Disk drives may be damaged by installing this card at an angle with the gold fingers of the card touching more than one connecting pin in the connector.

If you are using a II or II +, adjust the cable to lie flat as it passes out of the back of the computer as shown. When the lid is installed, it will clamp down on the cable and act as strain relief. If you have a IIe, the cables pass through one of the removable openings in the back of the

FIGURE 1.8 Disk drive cable placement.

computer and a strain relief clamp is mounted in place as in the photo. The disk drive(s) may be set beside or on top of the Apple.

Tape Recorders. The best advice for those who would consider using a tape recorder to store and save programs is don't. Tape recorders may seem to be an attractive means for storing programs because they are relatively inexpensive and are often already available. However, cassette systems are always slow and usually unreliable.

The Apple was originally shipped with demonstration cassette tapes and cassette cables. This practice was subsequently discontinued. Variations in the recorder's volume, tone, head alignment, and speed can cause the loss of valuable programs. Tapes which stick, drag, stretch, or break can mean disaster for the computer user. Even under ideal conditions, tape programs are relatively slow to load. Long programs may take five minutes or more. If you must use a tape recorder, consider it a temporary measure and start saving for a disk drive.

A good quality cassette recorder is a necessity. The recorder can be any brand provided it has a counter and jacks for a microphone and earphones. Make sure that the heads are clean and properly aligned.

The recorder should be connected to the *in* and *out* ports described earlier in this chapter, which are located at the rear right of the computer. Connections are the same for the IIe, II+, and II. Use twin RCA cables. Earlier Apples were shipped with these. If your Apple does not have them, they can be purchased at any Radio Shack store. These are the same inexpensive cables often used in stereo systems. Make certain that the cable you plug into the *out* port on the Apple is connected to the microphone jack on the tape recorder. The other cable should connect the *in* port of your Apple to the jack labeled *headphone, ear,* or *speaker* on your recorder.

Printers. If you have a printer, you also must have an Apple-compatible interface card to allow your computer to talk to the printer. There are many types of printers and interface cards that will be discussed later. Connecting the printer to the computer is simple. There will be a flat or round cable connected to the interface card, which connects to a plug on the back of your printer. The card is placed in one of the slots (conventionally, slot one) in your Apple, in the same manner as the disk controller card. Most printers must be plugged in to an electrical plug and turned on independently of the Apple.

The 80-Column Board. The IIe is made to work with an inexpensive Apple 80-column adapter. This allows the IIe to display 80 characters of print per line like more expensive business computers. The normal display is 40 characters per line. The IIe has a special slot where the 80-column card can be installed. This slot is on the left of the motherboard near the keyboard. (See Figure 1.2.) The II + s and IIs also may have 80-column boards added to them. To install an 80-column board in a II or II + , place it in slot three as you would connect the disk drive and printer interfaces.

When you are finished making the connections, replace the cover, place your disk drive or tape recorder beside the computer, and put your TV on top of or beside the computer. Plug in the computer, TV, and printer, if you have one. You are now ready to learn to use the keyboard to communicate with your Apple.

USING THE KEYBOARD

If you have made all of the connections previously described, you are ready to practice typing on the keyboard. If you have a disk drive with your computer, place the disk labeled "system master," which came with your Apple, into drive one with the slot facing forward and label up. Close the door to the drive. Turn on your television set or monitor. If you are using a regular TV, don't forget to set it to the channel used by your modulator. Next, turn on your Apple with the rocker switch located on the back left of the computer. Your Apple should beep at you and you should see the red light on the disk drive come on (if you have one). The disk drive will make some whirring and clicking noises, and momentarily you will see a screen display titled SYSTEM MASTER.

If you aren't using a disk drive, the screen will simply display APPLE II at the top with a blinking square called the cursor below it on the left side of the screen.

When you have reached this point, you are now ready to learn to use the computer keyboard. If you don't see this display, turn the computer off and carefully recheck the connections and instructions. The Apple II and II + have identical keyboards, but the IIe has a somewhat different keyboard. We will look at these separately. It is only necessary to read the section describing the keyboard for the Apple model you have.

The II and II + Keyboard

The power light located at the lower left of the keyboard is just an indicator light. It glows when your Apple is on. It is not an on-off switch. The power switch is located on the left rear of the machine where it is more likely to be away from harm.

The Apple keyboard looks much like a standard typewriter keyboard with a few differences. You only get capital letters on the video screen with the II + (unless you purchase a lowercase adapter for it). **SHIFT**

FIGURE 1.9 The Apple II+ keyboard.

keys are located on both sides of the keyboard. These are used to obtain alternate characters from some of the keys. The top row of keys contains numbers and symbols. Pressing any of these keys together with the **SHIFT** key will give you the symbol shown on the top of the key. There is one exception — the G key. The G key has the word **BELL** on it, but pressing **Shift/G** does not put **BELL** on the screen. Instead, it produces a beep. Pressing the shift key with a key that does not have an "upper" symbol on it has no effect with the exception of the M key. **SHIFT/M** produces a left hand square bracket like this,]. The key labeled **CTRL** is the control key and is used as an alternate shift key, permitting some of the keys to have a third function. However, the control key does not place a new character on the screen. Instead, a certain action is performed. **CTRL/G**, for example, will produce a beep, as previously pointed out. (Even though the word bell is printed on the G key, the sound produced doesn't sound like a bell.) Other control characters will be discussed later. Try typing a few sentences. Try the **CTRL/G** and using the shift to produce the alternate characters. If you press the **RETURN**, your Apple will present you with a **"SYNTAX ERROR"** message. Ignore this for now. This will be explained later. You can't hurt the computer by typing on it, so don't be afraid to experiment.

There are two differences which often cause trouble between the Apple keyboard and most typewriters. One is that you cannot use the lower case

L for a 1. The character 1 is located at the top left of the keyboard. Another problem is the 0. The letter O and the number 0 (zero) are similar on most typewriters, but you cannot use the capital letter O to represent a zero on the Apple. The method for keeping zeros distinct on the Apple, and on most other computers, is to place a slash through the zeros. The keyboard and the video screen make this distinction apparent. Try typing some Os and 0s on your Apple and see.

Above the **CONTROL** key is a key labeled **ESC**. This stands for escape and is used to perform special functions. The escape key is not used with other keys as are the **CONTROL** and **SHIFT** keys and it produces no characters on the screen. Some programs use the escape key to stop the program to return to a menu screen, or to perform other special tasks. Pressing **ESC** followed by **SHIFT/P** will clear the screen.

On the right side of the keyboard are a few more strange keys. The arrow keys move the cursor, the blinking square on the screen, to the right or left. The left arrow is useful for correcting typing errors. Just move the cursor to the mistake and type over it. The old letter will disappear and the new one will appear in its place. As the right arrow key is pressed, it recopies any characters that the cursor passes over. More will be explained about these keys when we get to programming. Above the left arrow is the repeat key labeled **REPT**. Holding down **REPT** and any other key will cause the key's character to appear repeatedly on the screen. Pressing the **REPT** simultaneously with an arrow key will allow your cursor to zip across the screen. Try experimenting with these keys on your Apple.

Next to the **REPT** is the **RETURN** key. Pressing this key will cause the cursor to return to the left side of the screen on the next line much like it does on a typewriter. It also issues a special message to the computer to enter any information you have typed on the screen into the computer's memory. **To enter any command, or other information, you must always press RETURN.**

Finally, there is the all-important **RESET** key. Pressing this key will "kill" whatever program you happen to be running or writing! Its position above the **RETURN** key makes accidental resets a potential hazard. The Apple provides a safeguard against accidental resets. A small switch located inside the computer can be set to disable the **RESET** key.

Lift the cover again, and look just under the front center edge of the computer to see it. Setting this switch to the left will cause the **RESET** key to work only when it is pressed together with the **CONTROL** key. Unless you have a good reason for not doing so, it is highly recommended that you set this switch to the left. Otherwise, much grief can ensue if you accidentally hit the **RESET** key and kill a program. Resetting also reboots (reinstalls) the disk operating system (DOS) if you are using a disk system.

Functionally, resetting is the same as turning the computer off and then on again. All the programs and data stored in the RAM are erased and DOS is reloaded into the Apple's memory.

The IIe Keyboard

The green Apple light on the bottom left of the keyboard is the indicator light on the IIe. It glows when your Apple is turned on. It is not an on/off switch. If you are using a disk drive, insert the system master disk, with the slot forward and the label up, and close the drive's door. The power switch is located on the left rear of the machine. If you have made all of the connections previously described, you are ready to turn on the computer and get started. When the cursor, the blinking square, appears you are ready to begin.

The IIe has a 63-character keyboard with uppercase and lowercase letter capability. All keys have auto repeat. Holding a key down causes the character to repeat; this is especially helpful when fast cursor movement is needed. **SHIFT** keys are located on either side of the keyboard, just like on a typewriter. Holding one of them down and then pressing a letter key produces a capital letter on the screen. Pressing a letter key without the **SHIFT** produces a lowercase letter.

SHIFT keys also produce special alternate characters when pressed simultaneously with keys that have two symbols on them. The top row of

FIGURE 1.10 The Apple IIe keyboard.

characters contain both numbers and symbols. For example, pressing any of these together with the **SHIFT** key will produce the symbol shown on the top of the key.

The key labeled **CONTROL** is used as an alternate shift key, permitting some of the keys to have a third function. However, instead of placing a character on the screen, a certain action is performed when the keys are pressed. **CONTROL/G**, for example, will produce a beep. **CONTROL/P** will clear the screen. Try typing a few sentences. Try the **CONTROL/G** and use the **SHIFT** key to produce alternate characters. If you press **RE-TURN**, your Apple will present you with a **"SYNTAX ERROR"** message. Ignore this for now. This will be explained later. You can't hurt your Apple by typing on it, so don't be afraid to experiment.

There are two differences between the Apple keyboard and most typewriters that often cause trouble. One difference is that you cannot use the lowercase L for a 1. The character 1 is located on the top row of keys next to the key labeled **ESC**. Another potential problem is the 0. The letter O and the number 0 (zero) can be used interchangeably on many typewriters, but you cannot use the capital letter O to represent a zero on the Apple. The zero is located next to the 9 key on the top row of keys. The method used to keep zeros distinct on the Apple, and on many other computers, is to place a slash (/) through them. The keyboard and the video screen make this apparent. Try typing some Øs and Os on your Apple.

The key labeled **ESC** on the upper left of the keyboard is the escape key. It is used to perform special functions in some programs. It is not used with other keys like the **CONTROL** and **SHIFT** keys and it does not place characters on the screen. Pressing the **ESC** will have no effect unless you are using a program which specifically calls for it. Some programs use the escape key to exit the program, return to a menu, or perform other special tasks. Pressing **ESC** followed by **SHIFT/P** will clear the screen.

On the right side of the keyboard are several more strange-looking keys. The four keys with arrows on them are used to move the blinking square cursor around the screen. The arrow keys are useful in correcting typing mistakes. Just move the cursor to the mistake and type over the mistake with the correct character. The old letter will disappear and the new one will appear in its place. Try it and see for yourself.

Above the right **SHIFT** key is the key labeled **RETURN**. This is a special key. Pressing it will cause the cursor to return to the left side of the screen on the next line much like it does on a typewriter, but it also issues a special message to the computer to enter any information you have typed into the computer's memory. **To enter any command or other information, you must always press RETURN.**

There are keys with a picture of an Apple on them which are located on either side of the space bar. There is an "open Apple" (left) and "closed Apple" (right) key. They perform the same functions as the game paddle buttons and will be covered later. These are useful in games and some other programs which give them special meanings. They also are used to initiate a self-test for your Apple which will be discussed later. Pressing these keys now will have no effect.

Pressing the **CAPS LOCK** key located on the lower left of the keyboard locks the letter keys into uppercase mode so that capital letters will be produced without use of the **SHIFT** key. The number and symbol keys are not affected by the **CAPS LOCK**. That is, with the **CAPS LOCK** set, the 4 key will produce a 4, not the $. Try it and see. The **CAPS LOCK** key should normally be kept down in the locked position.

The **RESET** key is recessed and located above and to the right of the main keyboard. It will not work unless it is pressed together with the **CONTROL** key, a move called **CONTROL/RESET**. Resetting is functionally the same as turning the computer off and then on again. Pressing the **RESET** key at the wrong time on the II+ and II computers could be catastrophic, because whatever program you happened to be working with would be lost from the computer's memory. Because of the location of the **RESET** on the IIe keyboard and the fact that it can be used only with the **CONTROL** key, accidental resets are unlikely. If you press **CONTROL/RESET** at this time, you will see the screen clear, your disk will whirr momentarily (if you have one), and the Apple's memory will be wiped clean. You will then be ready to start anew.

The **DELETE** key, on the upper right part of the keyboard, is used when your Apple is working as a terminal that lets you communicate with a larger computer and with some programs that are written to take advantage of its capabilities. **DELETE** works like a destructive backspace. Pressing it will delete the character to the left of the cursor, but only in those programs which use **DELETE**. Pressing the **DELETE** key at this time will have no effect.

The **TAB** key, located below the **ESC** key on the left side of the keyboard, works like a tab on a typewriter and moves the cursor quickly to a predetermined place on the line being typed. Like the **DELETE** key, **TAB** only operates with programs specifically written to take advantage of it. Pressing it now will have no effect.

The IIe often is sold with the Apple 80-column card, so its use will be described here. Other 80-column cards that work with any of the Apple IIs also are available and these will be discussed in Chapter 3.

An 80-column card will allow your video to display 80 characters per line. A 40-character line display is normal for the Apple. The 40-column display gives larger print because there are fewer characters per line. An 80-column display is most useful in word processing applications. To change to 80 columns from 40 with the Apple 80-column board in place, type either PR#3 or IN#3 and press **RETURN**. To change from 80 columns back to 40, press **CONTROL/Q**. After you have turned on the 80-column display with IN#3, you can switch back to it from the 40-column mode with a **CONTROL/R**.

To demonstrate these procedures for those who have the 80-column card installed, type PR#3 and press **RETURN**, and then type the following line and press **RETURN**:

The quick brown fox jumped over the lazy dog.

Ignore the **SYNTAX ERROR** message that will appear on the screen. Now, hold down the **CONTROL** key and press the Q key. The sentence you typed will disappear and then reappear but in larger letters. To switch back to the original form, hold down **CONTROL** and press R.

HAVING SOME FUN

Once the connections and basic use of the keyboard have been mastered, you are ready to give your Apple's chips a little exercise.

First type **NEW** and press **RETURN**. The specifics of BASIC programming will be explained later. For now just type in the little program below exactly as it is listed. If you make a typing mistake before you press **RETURN**, use the back arrow key to move the cursor backward and then type the correct character. If you make a mistake after pressing **RETURN**, just retype the entire line. Always press **RETURN** after typing each line.

```
10  FOR X = 1 TO 100
20  PRINT X
30  NEXT X
```

Now type **RUN** and press **RETURN**.

What happens? You should have seen a series of numbers from one to one hundred appear in a column on the left side of the screen. This program instructs the computer to count to one hundred. The computer "executes" or runs the program when you tell it to **RUN**. Now type **LIST** and press **RETURN** to enter the command. You should see our program reappear on the screen. The program will remain in the computer's RAM until you turn the computer off, press the **CONTROL/RESET** key, or type **NEW** again. Now type the following new line 20.

```
20  PRINT "HELLO"
```

LIST your program again. It should look like this:

```
10  FOR X = 1 TO 100
20  PRINT "HELLO"
30  NEXT X
```

The old line 20 was erased and replaced by the new one. **RUN** our program now. What happens this time? It should display a series of HELLOS on the screen instead of numbers.

(photo 1.17)

Next add a blank space after the O in HELLO and a semicolon (;) to the end of line 20 by retyping it to look like this:

```
20  PRINT "HELLO ";
```

RUN the program again. What happens now? Hello will now be displayed continuously across the screen until the screen is filled. The semicolon prevents the automatic line feed which the Apple usually does after printing something.

Try experimenting with variations of this program. Substitute your name for HELLO or use numbers other than 100. Try typing a phrase or your name inside the quotation marks in line 20 instead of HELLO. Presto! You are now computing and programming.

More will be said about programming in Chapter 5. In the next chapter, we'll look at loading and saving programs using a disk drive or tape recorder and explore some neat things to do with the computer.

Chapter 2

Getting Your Apple
Up and Running

By this point you should have all your connections properly made and be generally familiar with use of the keyboard. If this is the case, you are no doubt ready to begin exploring the capabilities of the computer more seriously. First we'll look at the three modes in which the Apple can operate and then we'll discuss how to use disk drives and tape recorders to save and load programs. Several demonstration programs are included to help you put the Apple through its paces and have some fun.

APPLE A LA MODE

The Text Mode

The Apple can operate in three different modes: text, low-resolution graphics, and high-resolution graphics. The text display is what you see when you first turn your Apple on and begin to type. In the 40-column text mode, up to 39 characters may be displayed on each horizontal line. (The fortieth column is used for the carriage return and does not show on the screen.) Up to 79 characters may be placed on each line with the use of the 80-column card which was described in Chapter 1. Twenty-four vertical lines fill the video screen. Unless you buy a lowercase adapter, all letters are uppercase only on the II+ and II. The IIe will display both lowercase letters and capitals if you don't press the **CAPS LOCK** key. The text mode is generally considered the normal mode, and is used when you write programs, enter information during programs, and when you want to display print information. The little programs described in Chapter 1 operate in the text mode. Here's another sample program. Type **NEW**, press **RETURN**, and then type this program on your Apple exactly as it is listed. Be careful to type the program exactly and remember to press **RETURN** after each line. If you make a typing error, use the back arrow to back up and then retype correctly. If you find an error in a line after it has been entered, just retype the line. When you are finished, read on to see how it works.

OLD FOLKS PROGRAM:

```
1    TEXT:HOME
10   PRINT "HELLO, I'M THE APPLE COMPUTER.
     WHAT'S YOUR NAME?"
20   INPUT NAME$:PRINT
30   PRINT "HI ";NAME$ ;" LET'S HAVE SOME FUN
     TOGETHER."
40   PRINT:PRINT "HOW OLD ARE YOU (IN YEARS)?"
50   INPUT YEARS
60   DAYS = YEARS * 365
70   PRINT NAMES$;", YOU HAVE LIVED FOR ";DAYS;" DAYS
     AS OF YOUR LAST BIRTHDAY."
80   PRINT "MAKES YOU FEEL OLD DOESN'T IT."
90   PRINT:PRINT "BYE NOW."
100  END
```

A program is a set of instructions which tell the computer what to do. This program asks for your age, calculates the number of days in those years, and prints out the result. The rest is window dressing. Once entered, the program will remain in the computer's memory until you erase it by typing **NEW**, press **RESET**, or turn your computer off. When you type **RUN**, the computer begins to follow the instructions of the program.

Let's look at how the program works. Line 1 does a little housekeeping for us. It sets the text mode and clears the screen. Line 10 is a **PRINT** statement like the ones in the programs in Chapter 1. **PRINT** statements cause whatever appears inside the quotation marks to appear on the screen when the program is **RUN**. Line 20 introduces a command that we have not used before — an **INPUT** statement. This tells the computer that information is to be entered by the user from the keyboard. In this case the **INPUT** information is a name. When the program is **RUN**, it will halt at this point and wait for you to type your name. (Remember, you must always press **RETURN** to enter information into the computer.) The extra **PRINT** in lines 20, 40, and 90 simply causes a line to be skipped or left blank when the program is run. Line 30 puts several items together and prints them out. This is called concatenation. **NAME$** is a variable which stores your name. The dollar sign indicates that the information to be entered consists of alphabetic characters rather than numbers. Line 40 is another **PRINT** statement which asks you for more information — your age. **YEARS** is the variable name assigned by the **INPUT** statement in line 50. No dollar sign is needed here because the information requested is a number. Line 60 does a little math. It instructs the computer to multiply your age in years times 365 (the number of days in one year). The result is the number of days which you have lived (up to your last birthday). This figure is printed out in line 70 in a sentence format. Lines 80 and 90 are both more **PRINT** statements. Line 100 signifies the end of the program.

Don't be concerned if this all seems a little difficult to grasp. More will be explained about programming in Chapter 5. Experiment with the program. Can you think of ways to modify it to make it more interesting?

Low-Resolution Graphics

FIGURE 2.1 A low resolution (low res) graphics display.

One of the most popular features of the Apple is its ability to produce neat graphics. This means that neat games, fancy graphs and charts, and cute pictures are all possible. Two types of graphics are available — low-resolution and high-resolution. Low-resolution graphics are drawn on an invisible 40×40 grid on the video screen. Sixteen different colors may be used. Colors are represented in programs by numbers. Graphics may

be still pictures or they may include moving elements. The normal low-resolution graphics mode includes space for four lines of text at the bottom of
the video screen. The low-resolution grid and the colors available by
number are shown in Figure 2.2.

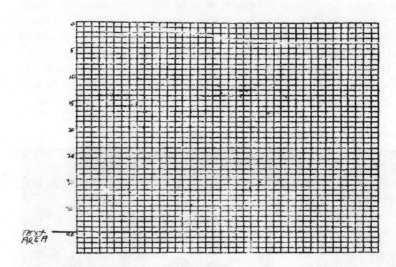

FIGURE 2.2 The Apple II low res graphics grid is 40 × 40.

Apple Low-Resolution Color Table:

0	black	8	brown
1	magenta	9	orange
2	dark blue	10	gray
3	purple	11	pink
4	dark green	12	green
5	grey	13	yellow
6	medium blue	14	aqua
7	light blue	15	white

The next program demonstrates low-resolution graphics. Type **NEW** to
let your Apple know that you are beginning a new program and enter this
program and **RUN** it.

```
10 GR: HOME
20 COLOR = 2
30 FOR X = 1 TO 40
40 VLIN 0,39 AT X
50 NEXT X
```

The result should be a nice blue screen. The GR in line 10 tells the Apple to change to the low-resolution graphics mode. Line 20 sets the color to blue. Line 30 begins a "loop" which is to be repeated 40 times. Line 40 draws a vertical line at point X from the horizontal grid point 0 to horizontal grid point 39. This is then repeated 40 times, enough to color the entire screen by drawing vertical lines until the screen is full. You will notice that we started with 0 instead of 1 in drawing our vertical lines. Computers usually use 0 for the first digit. Hence, the forty columns are labeled 0 through 39 instead of 1 through 40.

The screen will remain blue until you do something to change it. Type **TEXT:HOME** and press **RETURN**. This should clear your screen. **LIST** your program again.

Next add the following new lines to the program:

    60 COLOR = 9
    70 VLIN 0,39 AT 20
    80 HLIN 0,39 AT 20

RUN the program again. This time you should have a blue screen with a red + on it. Line 60 changes the color to orange. Line 70 draws a vertical line across the screen at horizontal line 20, which is the center of the screen. Line 80 introduces a new command **HLIN**, which draws horizontal lines. This one goes across the screen at vertical point 20. Experiment with the program. Can you draw a box? Can you change the colors? Can you draw other shapes?

High-Resolution Graphics

High-resolution graphics are much more detailed than are low-resolution graphics, but only eight colors may be used. As with low-resolution graphics, high-resolution graphics are drawn on an invisible grid. The high-resolution grid is 280 units across by 160 units down. The horizontal coordinates start at 0 on the left of the screen and end with 279 on the right. Likewise, the vertical coordinates go from 0 at the top of the screen to 159 at the bottom. High-resolution graphics commands are similar to low-resolution graphics commands with the addition of an H (for high-resolution). **HGR** tells the Apple that you want to use the high-resolution graphics mode. The only instruction for plotting in high-resolution graphics is **HPLOT**. Lines can be plotted from one grid coordinate point to another without regard to whether the lines drawn are vertical, horizontal, or diagonal. The program below demonstrates the Apple's high-resolution graphics. Type **NEW**, enter the program below and **RUN** it. Can you tell what it does before you run it?

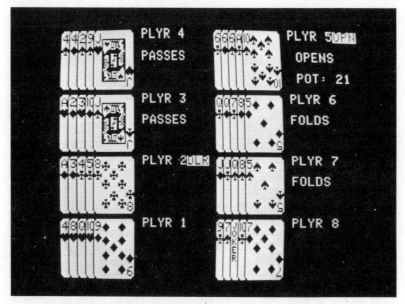

FIGURE 2.3 A high resolution display from a popular game.

```
10 HGR
20 HCOLOR = 2
30 HPLOT 0,0 TO 279,0 TO 279,159 TO 0,159 TO 0,0
40 HOME
50 PRINT :PRINT "HI-RES FRAME"
```

The program above will draw a violet frame around your screen. Lines 40 and 50 use the four text lines allowed at the bottom of the screen to title our graphic.

The additions to the program which follows will turn your Apple into a sketching screen on which you can draw using your game paddles. Type these additions into your Apple without killing the original program, **RUN** the new program, and experiment with the paddle controls. (Refer to Chapter 1 for information on connecting the game paddles if you do not have them connected.)

```
 60   HCOLOR = 5
 70   X = PDL (0)
 80   Y = PDL (1)
 90   IF Y> 159 THEN Y = 159
100   HPLOT X,Y
110   GOTO 70
```

Presto! We have a sketch pad. Here's how it works. Line 60 changes the color to orange. Lines 70 and 80 instruct the computer to read the values of X and Y supplied by the game paddles. Line 90 is included because the paddles can return values up to 255, and the Y coordinate would be off the screen if its value were greater than 159. Line 100 plots a pixel (short for picture element) at the coordinate values supplied by the two paddles. Line 110 keeps the program running in an "endless loop." As you move the control on the paddle marked 0, the horizontal value being read will change. Paddle One will vary the vertical coordinate. By using the two paddles together, you can draw shapes. To stop the program press **CTRL/C**. **RUN** the program again and you have a clean screen to start again.

Programs may use any one, or all three, of these modes — text, low-resolution graphics, or high-resolution graphics. However, only one mode may normally be used at a time. In other words, typed text words may not be included with graphics except in the bottom four lines, and high- and low-resolution graphics cannot be mixed on the same visual display. Programming in all three modes is explained in more detail in Chapters 5 and 6.

USING A DISK DRIVE

FIGURE 2.4 The Apple disk drive II.

Care and Feeding of Disks

Using a disk drive is much quicker and easier than using a cassette recorder. Disk drives and diskettes are, however, delicate, and must be handled with care. Since the disk is a magnetic medium, care must be taken to keep it away from magnetic fields such as those of electric motors or the information they store can be erased or damaged. We once accidentally laid a screwdriver with a magnetic tip on a disk and found our programs would no longer load. The disk also should be kept free of dust and fingerprints. Keep the disk in its protective envelope when not in use. Do not touch the portion of the disk exposed through the slot in its protective cover. The disk is slightly flexible, but don't bend it excessively. Disks are also heat sensitive. If you leave a disk on the dashboard of your car for very long in the summer, all you'll end up with is a small, warped frisbee. Disks should be stored vertically in a file box or in a notebook with vinyl pockets. Don't leave disks lying about or set heavy items on top of them.

Five-and-a-quarter-inch disks, or diskettes as they are frequently called, can hold a tremendous amount of information — more than 1,146,000 bits of information. (A bit may represent a 1 or a 0.) Eight bits are called a byte and represent a single letter, number, or other character. An individual bit, however, occupies only a tiny spot on the disk's surface. An invisible scratch or fingerprint, therefore, can cause errors. When writing on the little disk labels, always use a felt tip pen and don't press down hard. Pressure from a pen may crease and damage the disk. Another hint — use only high quality diskettes. Most brands of diskettes are of a quality which will provide good service on the Apple. However, it pays to avoid questionable products. Good diskettes will be "guaranteed" — that is to say, they will be replaced or your money refunded if they fail. Good brands also are "certified," which means they have been electronically tested and found to have a coating free of errors. Brands which do not clearly state these two qualities, or which do not clearly bear the name of the manufacturer should be avoided. The Apple Disk II drive unit uses what is known as a single-density format. Disks which are certified as single-density quality will provide adequate reliability. Some other disk drives require more expensive double-density disks. These also may be used on the Disk II drive even though they are not required. With good care, a quality disk will last for years of normal use. It should be noted, however, that disks will eventually wear out. Thus it pays to make back-up second copies of valuable programs you use a great deal.

Inserting The Disk

The diskette should be inserted into the drive unit with the label upwards and the oval slot entering the drive first. Disks may be inserted before the computer is turned on or when the computer is in operation. However, **never remove or insert disks when the disk drive light is on or your programs may be damaged or lost.** Open the door on the drive unit by lifting upward and inserting the disk gently. Push it all the way in, and close the little door.

Booting the Disk

For your Apple to communicate with the drive unit, the DOS program must be added to the computer's memory. Adding the DOS to your Apple is called "booting the system." The Apple II was not originally designed to operate with a disk unit so it does not include a DOS program in the machine's ROM memory as do some other computers. The disk operating system is included on the system master diskette which comes with the Disk II unit. DOS also may be included on any other disk. Commercial programs on disk usually have DOS as well. You may add DOS to disks of programs which you write by using the "Master Create" program which is also on the System Master Disk that comes with your disk drive.

There are several ways to boot DOS. One way is simply to turn your Apple off, insert a disk which has DOS on it into the disk drive, and turn it on again. When you do this, the drive's red light comes on and you hear some whirring noises. In a few moments, the drive will settle down, the light will go off, and you will be ready to write or load programs. Another way to boot DOS is to type the command **PR#6**, and press **RETURN** with a disk in the drive. Pressing the reset key also has the same effect. **Caution: Booting DOS will erase any program currently in the Apple's RAM.** Once DOS has been installed it will remain quietly hidden in your Apple's RAM until you turn off the computer or press **CONTROL/ RESET**. You may change disks or load new programs without rebooting (loading the DOS back into RAM).

Loading And Saving Programs

Once the DOS has been booted, you are ready to load a program. To do this, you enter the command **LOAD** followed by the program name. Then press **RETURN.** When you do this, you will see the disk's red light come on and the drive will whirr again. When it settles down, you may type the command **RUN** and your program will execute or **RUN**.

To see what programs are on a disk, you may enter the command **CATALOG**, and a listing of the programs which are on the disk will appear on your screen. The command **RUN** followed by a program name will both **LOAD** and **RUN** the program you have selected.

The letter to the right of each listing stands for the language in which the program is written. Languages available for the Apple are Applesoft

Basic (A), Integer Basic (I), Fortran (F), Pascal (P), and Binary or machine language (B). Text files (T) are not programs but files of data used by programs. The numbers to the right of the language code indicate the units of memory which the program occupies on the disk. The larger the number, the larger the program.

Several programs useful in programming are included on the system master. Another disk labeled Sample Programs comes with the Apple IIe. Some of these programs were also included with the II+ and II on the system master disk. On it are several neat demonstration programs. Color Test is a nice program for demonstrating low-resolution graphics. Entering the command **RUN** COLOR TEST will cause that program to **LOAD** and **RUN**. Little Brick is a paddle game on the sample program disk, in which you try to knock down walls of colored bricks using a bouncing ball (or bouncing brick). Biorhythm forecasts your immediate future in terms of your mental, emotional, and physical well-being based on your age and birthdate. For a complete description of programs on the system master, and sample programs disks, see the DOS Manual which comes with the Disk II drive or which is available from your Apple dealer. Try running some of these programs. They are easy and fun.

Saving programs on a disk is just as easy as loading them. When you have written or loaded a program you wish to save on a disk, enter the command **SAVE** together with a program name. You may name a program anything you wish as long as it begins with a letter and is no more than 30 characters long. Using short names will minimize the likelihood of typing errors when loading and running programs. A summary of the basic DOS commands, which you will need to operate the disk drive are given here.

TABLE 1. Basic DOS Commands

Command	Function
CATALOG	Displays the list of programs and files on the disk currently in the drive. If more than one disk drive is in use, the addition of a drive number specifies which catalog is to be displayed. For example: CATALOG,D2 displays the catalog on drive number 2.
INIT + program name	Formats a blank or used diskette to the Apple DOS format and assigns the program named as the greeting program. **INIT** will erase everything on the disk so that it can be reused. New disks must be

"initialized" before they can be used on your Apple. The command **INIT** HELLO will reformat the disk currently in the drive and place the program in memory on it.

LOAD + program name

Loads the program into the Apple but does not execute it. The command **LOAD** COPYA will load the program titled COPYA from the system master disk but will not run it.

RUN + program name

Loads and executes the program named from the disk currently in the drive. The command **RUN** COPYA will **LOAD** and **RUN** the program titled COPYA from the system master disk.

SAVE + program name

Places the program currently in the Apple's memory on the disk with the name given, and overwrites any program with the same name currently on the disk. **SAVE** FACE saves the program currently in the computer's memory on the disk and names it FACE.

DELETE + program name

Permanently erases the program named from the disk. **DELETE** FACE permanently erases the program titled FACE from the disk.

RENAME + program name, new name

Changes the name of the first named program to the new one given. The command **RENAME** FACE, SAMPLE changes the name of the program in the disk directory but does not alter the program itself.

LOCK + program name

Protects the named program from being deleted, renamed, or revised and places an asterisk(*) beside the program when listed in the catalog. Use **LOCK** to guard against accidentally erasing a valuable program. The command **LOCK** SAMPLE will secure the SAMPLE program.

UNLOCK + program name

Unlocks the program named. **UNLOCK** SAMPLE will remove the lock placed on the program by the **LOCK** command.

PR#6

Boots DOS; that is, the DOS is loaded into the memory of the Apple. The command **PR#6** will cause the RAM to be cleared and will **LOAD** and **RUN** the greeting program on the disk.

PR#1

Sends commands to the printer if one is connected to slot #1. After the command **PR#1** is entered, no apparent action takes place, but if a printer is connected and turned on subsequent **RUN** and **LIST** commands will cause the output to be printed on paper.

BLOAD,BRUN,BSAVE   Performs the same functions as **LOAD**, **RUN**, **SAVE** for binary (machine language) programs.

USING A TAPE RECORDER

For those who must use a cassette tape recorder, you will likely find loading and saving programs slow and problem prone. There are only two commands for the tape recorder — **LOAD** and **SAVE**. No program names are used. To load a program from a cassette tape, first connect the recorder in the manner described in Chapter 1. Next insert the program tape into the recorder. Make sure the program you wish to load is on the face-up side of the tape. Tapes may have information on both sides. Now rewind the tape and press the counter button so that zeros are shown in the little counter window on the recorder. Sometimes several programs will be on each side of a cassette. Cassettes you buy will have the names of the programs they contain in a user's guide which comes with the tape. If the program you wish to use is not the first one on the tape, advance the tape with the fast forward or cue control until the number corresponding to the location of the desired program is shown in the counter window. Set the volume and tone level on the recorder to the midpoints.

Enter the command **LOAD** and press **RETURN**. The blinking cursor disappears. The computer is now looking for information to be loaded through the tape port. Press the Play button on the recorder and wait. In a moment, you should hear a beep from your Apple. This indicates that all is well and that the program is being loaded. Once the loading is complete, another beep will be heard and the cursor will reappear. It may take anywhere from several seconds to several minutes, depending on the length of the program, to complete the loading process. When the program is loaded, press the Stop button on the recorder and enter the command **RUN**. The program should now **RUN**.

ERR

The computer has no way of knowing whether or not a tape recorder is actually connected to it or if connections are made improperly, so the cursor will disappear after you type **LOAD** regardless of whether a tape recorder is connected or not. If you type **LOAD** when there is no recorder in place, the cursor will disappear while your Apple looks in vain for the program it is to receive from the tape. Eventually the cursor will return to the screen in disappointment and the message ERR for error will be displayed.

You may see an **ERR** message even if you have your recorder connected properly. If this happens, adjust your volume to a higher level, rewind your tape to the beginning of your program and try again. It also may be necessary to adjust the tone on your recorder. Several attempts may be necessary before you find the combination of settings your Apple likes. If the tape sticks or drags or if the speed or head alignment of your recorder is a little off, your programs will not load and you will continue to receive **ERR** messages. Higher-than-normal volume levels and tone controls set toward treble tend to produce better results.

Sometimes the same program will be recorded on your tape several times. In case one copy refuses to load after several tries, try another one.

Saving Programs on Tape

To save a program you have written, first insert a blank cassette into your recorder, rewind it to the beginning, and press the counter reset button. Simultaneously, press the Record and Play buttons on the recorder. Next enter the command **SAVE** and press **RETURN**. The cursor should now disappear. In a few seconds, you should hear a beep as the computer sends the program to the tape. When the program has been saved, the Apple will beep again and the cursor will return to the screen. Saving the program does not erase it from your computer's memory. It is a good idea to repeat the save procedure a second time at a different location on the tape or on a new tape just in case there is a problem with the first copy of the program. The only sure way to verify that your program has been properly saved is to reload it back into the Apple.

Use short, good quality tapes. Cassettes are unreliable enough without asking for more trouble by using cheap tapes. Computer programs take up little space on a cassette tape so use short tapes. Placing many programs on one long tape will cause you to take more time to locate the program you desire. A long tape with many programs also increases the risk of losing programs if the tape is damaged.

Trouble Shooting Cassette Tapes

If you have a program that refuses to load, first recheck the cable connections. Make sure that one cable connects the *in* port on the Apple to the speaker jack on the recorder. The other cable should connect the *out* port of the Apple to the microphone jack of the recorder.

If the cable connections are OK, unplug the Apple's cables from the recorder. Advance or rewind the tape to the location of the program and press the Play button. You should hear a high-pitched tone, which will continue for several seconds, followed by what sounds like static. If you do not hear these sounds, the program is not where you thought it was. Use the Rewind, Fast Forward and Play buttons until you locate the tone.

Once you have found the tone, reconnect the tape recorder to your Apple and try again.

If the above procedures don't help, try cleaning the recorder's tape heads. Cotton swabs with alcohol will do the job. If you suspect head alignment problems, take your recorder to the repair shop or refer to the tape recorder owner's manual to align them.

USING A PRINTER

If you have a printer, programs may be **RUN** or listed to the printer as well as to your video screen. A printer is a very handy accessory for your Apple. If you write programs, you will find a hard copy or paper printout of your program listing invaluable to study, "debug," and document your programs. Programs that produce reports, lists, tables, and the like will, of course, need a printer to be effective.

If the printer is connected as described in Chapter 1, the command **PR#1** will instruct the Apple to send information to it. Once **PR#1** has been entered, all **PRINT** instructions will be printed out on the printer as well as on the video screen. Printers take more time to print than do video displays, so be prepared to wait a little longer for your programs to **RUN**. Everything will continue to be printed out on the printer until you stop it with the command **PR#0**. Most printers also have an on/off switch which must be turned on for the printer to operate. Printers without graphics capability will not be able to reproduce Apple graphics symbols. When running a program that includes graphics on a non-graphics printer, usually the graphics symbols simply will not be shown on the printout, while regular text characters will be displayed normally.

To try out your printer, enter **NEW** to clear out your old program and then reenter the "old folks" program from the beginning of Chapter 2, or another sample program. Turn on your printer, and then type **PR#1** and press **RETURN**. Now **RUN** your program. It should work just as it did before, but with the output printed on paper as well as displayed on the video screen. **LIST** your program. It will be printed on the printer. Experiment with your printer. To turn the printer off, enter **PR#0**.

It is not possible to include a detailed description of printer operation here because of the wide variety of printers available for use with the Apple. Printers differ greatly in their speed, quality, and capabilities. Printers are discussed and described in greater detail in Chapter 3.

Now that we have the basic Apple down pat, we'll next take a look at the wide assortment of accessories and add-ons which help to make your Apple a powerful and versatile computer.

Chapter 3

Popular Accessories and What They Can Do for You

A vast array of devices are available that plug into your Apple and enhance its capabilities. More devices are made for the Apple than for any other microcomputer. This helps make the Apple the most versatile of the small computers, but it can also mean a bewildering array of choices for the user. The most popular products available will be covered here. Prices, sources, and evaluations of the products are included along with a list of product manufacturers at the end of the chapter.

TELEVISIONS AND VIDEO MONITORS

Your Apple isn't much good without a means of viewing your input and output, so one of the first and most important accessories that you will need to purchase is a TV set or video monitor. Some small computers come with built-in video screens. The Apple does not. This gives Apple owners more flexibility in choosing the type of video unit that best suits their needs, but it also means that from the very beginning, informed choices are a must.

Using Regular TV Sets for Video Display

The least expensive type of video display is the ordinary TV set. By using the modulator described in Chapter 1, you can hook up your Apple to your home television set. However, most people soon find that having a computer hooked up to the family TV set is not very satisfactory. Who gets priority when the kids want to watch cartoons or the spouse wants to watch a movie? Staring at a 24-inch screen from a distance of eight inches while working at a computer can also cause eye strain. After a short time, the average Apple addict is likely to be found in a local department store examining small TVs.

TV screens of about 12 or 13 inches diagonally are the size most often used with small computers. A small black-and-white television can be purchased for less than $100 in almost any discount department store. Black-and-white TVs will not allow you to take advantage of the Apple's excellent color graphics capability, but may be well suited to other applications, such as word processing. Games and children's educational programs often make extensive use of graphics, and some are almost impossible to use if you can't tell the colors apart. Small color sets cost more — perhaps in the neighborhood of $300. Used TVs are an alternative. The first video display for my Apple was a used nine-inch color television purchased from a local pawn shop for $125. It is still working just fine. TVs will serve satisfactorily as computer video displays and can double as an additional television for the late show after a tiring evening of Space Invaders or VisiCalc. However, there are some drawbacks to using a standard TV as a video display. Some good alternatives are available.

Using a Video Monitor

If you spend many hours in front of your computer, you will want your video display to be of good quality to avoid eye strain. Video monitors are video display units which look like small TVs, but which have several important differences. Video monitors usually have a higher quality display than regular TVs. Characters are better defined and appear crisper.

Instead of black-and-white displays, monochrome (one-color) monitors designed for use with computers often display green characters. Amber screens, long popular in Europe, also are becoming popular in the U.S. Green and amber screens are easier on the eyes than black and white.

Video monitors do not need the modulator which is necessary when using regular TV sets. Monitors are connected to the Apple through a simple cable which plugs directly into both the computer and the television monitor. A monitor will probably get a better picture because the video signal is channeled directly into the picture making circuits of the unit without first passing through the channel tuner. In fact, most monitors do not have channel tuners. This means they can't receive your local TV stations. If you want monitor quality but you also want to be able to use the unit to watch regular TV, you will need a monitor/receiver. These will cost more.

Because regular TVs are so common and readily available, we will not discuss them further here. The reviews that follow cover some of the video monitors most often used with the Apple.

The Apple III Green Screen Monitor

This unit is sold by local computer stores. Don't let the III business bother you. It works just fine with any Apple. This is a fine little 13-inch green screen monitor. The only problem with it is that its price of about $200 is too high.

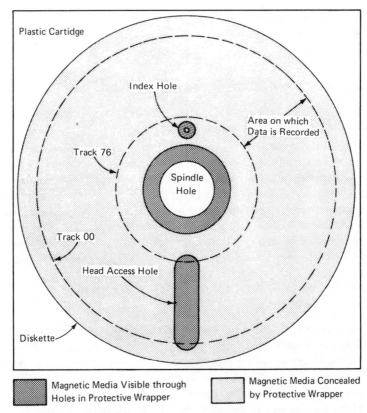

FIGURE 3.1 A diagram of a floppy disk.

The Zenith Hi-Res 12-Inch Green Monitor

This is a 12-inch green screen monitor that's hard to beat. It provides excellent picture quality and is manufactured by a company with a long and reputable history in the video business. It can be mail ordered or purchased locally in many computer stores. With a list price of $189, it is often discounted to less than $100.

Jade Amber or Green Monitors

Jade is an established supplier in computer components and accessories. Its 9-inch and 12-inch monitors cost about the same — $149 for amber and $139 for green. Both sizes have the same number of lines of resolution. The units are available by mail order or from Jade computer stores in California and Texas.

Amdek Color Monitors

This is probably the most popular small color monitor used with the Apple. It can either be purchased locally from computer stores or mail ordered from discount sources. The 13-inch Color I Monitor lists for about $389 and is often discounted to less than $320. It provides a good quality picture.

The NEC 12-Inch Color Monitor

This unit is approximately the same quality and price as the Amdek, but it has a slightly smaller screen. It includes a built-in speaker, while the Amdek does not. The speaker may or may not be an important feature. There is no way to directly connect your basic Apple to an external speaker, but some accessory units allow you to do this. Those not afraid to tinker can add an audio jack with a little solder and imagination. The speaker in the monitor is larger and of better quality than the one built into the Apple. Its volume can be adjusted. The Apple's speaker cannot be adjusted.

DISK DRIVES — DATA WAREHOUSES TO STORE YOUR PROGRAMS

The disk drive is the most popular accessory for your Apple. Because the Apple forgets everything in RAM when the power is turned off, some means of storing programs and other data is necessary. A disk drive is the most practical way to do this.

The Disk II drive made by Apple Computer was discussed in Chapter 1. There also are many other disk drive units which are compatible with the Apple. Some of these are almost identical in operation to the Disk II, while others have more storage capacity.

Hard disks are the most expensive and can store the most information. These units use a disk with a rigid recording surface.

Floppy disk systems use either 8" or 5¼" flexible disks and look like small 45 rpm records encased in a protective covering. The smaller 5¼" drives, like the Disk II, cost $200 to $500. The 8" drives cost from about $800 to $2,000, and can store at least three times as much data as the 5¼" drives.

Disk drives may be double or single density, double or single sided, and either soft or hard sectored. Single density means that data is not packed as densely on the disk as it is for double density systems. Single density systems are the least expensive.

Double-sided systems are simply those that use both sides of the disk. Soft sectored means that the data storage format of the disk is determined by the particular type of disk drive being used. Disk drives divide the data

FIGURE 3.2 A System Saver fan.

stored into "tracks." The more tracks there are, the more data the disk can store. A 40-track system can store several thousand data bytes more than a 37-track system. Hard-sectored disks use a series of holes in the disk surface to determine the format.

An important consideration in all of this disk business is compatibility. Almost all Apple software sold is on the Disk II format. It will not run on disk drives which have more tracks or double density. You should, therefore, have at least one Disk II or Disk II-compatible drive.

Lobo Drives

Lobo Drives International makes a family of Apple-compatible disk drives. Its top of the line 8″ hard disk unit is capable of storing eight megabytes of data. A megabyte is one million bytes. This unit sells for about $3,000. If that is more storage than you need, Lobo also has 8″ floppy drives. A single-sided 8″ drive can store 1.1 megabytes and sells for around $800. Lobo's double-sided, double-density drive units use both sides of the disk and store twice as much data as the single-sided versions for about $1,000.

Micro-sci also makes an assortment of Apple-compatible disk drives. Its least expensive model is the U-SCI which sells for less than $300 and, for all practical purposes, is identical to the Apple Disk II. It can be plugged directly into the Disk II controller card and used as the second drive. The U-SCI drive is as sturdy and reliable as the Disk II. In fact, this book was written on an Apple II+ computer with a U-SCI drive unit.

Many other companies also sell Apple-compatible drives as well as the interface cards used for connecting them to your computer.

FANS OR HOW TO AVOID BAKED APPLES

Overheating is a common problem for the Apple II and II+. Although it is less probable for the IIe, it can still cause problems. Heat is an enemy of computers because it can cause the tiny circuits inside the delicate chips to break. Too much heat also will cause chips to work their way out of the sockets, causing poor connections. Damaged or loose chips can cause all sorts of unpredictable and sometimes intermittent problems. Programs which once ran perfectly may fail or give error messages.

Fans are one means of fighting heat. The purpose of a fan, as you might expect, is to cool by creating a flow of air. If you have no accessories, you can probably get by without a fan. But if you have three or more accessory items such as disk drives or printer cards plugged into the accessory slots inside your Apple II or II+, you should get a fan to help fight heat buildup. The Apple IIe probably doesn't need a fan unless it has four or more accessories plugged into the slots. Make it a point to keep the openings located at the back and on the sides of your Apple clear of obstructions so that heat can escape and air can circulate inside the computer.

Apple Computer does not solder chips permanently to the motherboard. This makes repair and replacement easier but it also means that the heating and cooling process which occurs as you turn your Apple on and off may gradually force the chips loose from their sockets. Several little fans are made specifically for the Apple computer to help keep it cool.

The Superfan II

The Superfan II is one of the more popular fans for the Apple. It retails for less than $75 and is available from R/H Electronics. Superfan II fits on the side of your Apple without holes or screws and includes two extra 120V outlets. It is extremely quiet, includes an on/off switch with pilot light, and is finished in Apple beige.

System Saver

The System Saver is almost identical to the Superfan II with the addition of a surge protector which protects your computer system from voltage spikes. (Surge protectors will be discussed in more detail shortly.) It retails for less than $90 and is available from Kensington Microwave.

The Cool-Mark II

FIGURE 3.3 The Lemon surge protector.

The Cool-Mark II fan hides inside the Apple, unlike the System Saver and Superfan II which mount on the outside. It costs about $40, and is available from Mark Four Imports. The Cool-Mark carries a year warranty and seems to be a wise choice because it is inexpensive, quiet, and efficient.

Fans are much alike so shop for price, quiet operation, and pleasing appearance. Like most computer accessories, fans can be ordered by mail or purchased in most computer stores. Some folks we know have tried to improvise their own cooling systems with little fans taken from old slide projectors, tape recorders, or other small appliances. This is very risky. All electrical motors emit RF signals and magnetic fields, which can disrupt the operation of the computer. Fans that are not made to work with computers may not be properly shielded and may cause unpredictable problems such as erasure of disks, interference with the video picture, and failure of programs to load or operate properly. Improvising a cooling system just isn't worth the risk.

PROTECTION FROM ELECTRICAL SURGES
AND POWER LOSSES

Your Apple needs a constant, even flow of electrical current to operate properly. Drops or surges in the power supply can cause loss of data or even permanent damage to your program or the computer itself. Power surges, also known as glitches or spikes, are momentary surges of electrical voltage, and are the most serious electrical enemy of computers. Momentary drops in electrical voltage also can cause problems, but there is usually no permanent damage.

The Apple comes with a built-in power supply, which was described in Chapter 1. It protects the computer and the software, to some measure, against electrical power surges and tries to assure a constant, even flow of power. This may be all that you need. However, if your computer is going to be located in a building with an old electrical system or in a home with electrical appliances that draw large amounts of current, the additional protection of a surge protector is a good idea. Power companies also may be the culprits in producing power surges. Some power companies are more reliable than others. Even electrical storms can cause power spikes. You may be able to get by without a surge protector, but the small cost of protecting an expensive investment in hardware and software is well worth the piece of mind it brings.

Limes, Lemons, and Oranges

Electronic Protection Devices manufactures several devices which protect computers and other sensitive electronic equipment against power surges. These cost between $50 and $150. The Lemon surge protector is made for small computers primarily. It has six outlets and plugs into any standard 120-volt electrical outlet. You just plug whatever needs protecting into it, and electrical spikes will be blocked before they cause damage.

The Guardian Angel Power Source

This unit will not only protect your Apple from power surges, but it also will provide up to six minutes of standby power in the event of power failure. It can be connected to regular household 115 to 120-volt current, 220-volt circuits, or 12-volt DC so that you can compute from your car, boat, or RV by connecting it to the cigarette lighter. If these are important features to you, the $595 will be money well spent. The Guardian Angel can be ordered by mail or purchased from local computer stores.

PRINTERS

A printer is one of the most important and versatile accessories that you can add to your Apple computer system. If you write programs, a printed program listing is very useful for finding errors and making changes. Producing letters and manuscripts through word processing becomes practical with the addition of a printer. Printers also are useful for printing graphics, tables, lists, or lots of other things. Some programs require that a printer be attached to the computer for them to operate.

Choosing a printer is not an easy task. Today there are more than 200 printers available in the under $5,000 range, and 150 can be had for $3,000 or less. Even narrowing the field to $500 or less gives buyers a choice of at least 100 models. (Just two were available in 1979.) However, price is not the only variable. Consider print quality, print type, paper type, speed, noise, controls, graphics capability, interfacing, servicing, and longevity.

Longevity refers to the length of time that the unit can be expected to operate before it needs service. This is obviously extremely important, but is difficult to measure given that most makes and models of printers haven't been around long. You can make informed judgments based on the manufacturer's reputation and history, the design of the unit, and the number of moving parts.

Print Types

Basically, there are only two popular types today — dot matrix and fully formed character printers. A dot matrix printer uses a head made up of a group of tiny wires, which strike the ribbon as the print head moves across the page. Characters are formed from a matrix of dots caused by the impact of the wires on the paper through the ribbon. Although dot matrix printers today are a considerable improvement over those of just a few years ago, they still fall a bit short of what most people consider letter quality. Even the best dot matrix printers cannot produce characters as good as those of a typewriter. A printer which produces fully formed letters is sometimes called "letter quality," which means that it is suitable for most formal business correspondence. Essentially, the printed output is equivalent to that of an electric typewriter.

Letter quality printers usually form characters in one of two ways — type ball mechanisms like those on IBM electric typewriters, and the "daisy wheel," so called because it looks like a black plastic (or metal) daisy flower. (Actually, it looks more like a chrysanthemum.) This little four-inch diameter wheel has molded characters on the end of each "petal." It con-

FIGURE 3.4 A Daisy Wheel.

tinually spins when the printer is operating, and a print hammer strikes the correct characters to print. Print quality is judged by the printout. A comparison of printouts from several of the most popular printers is shown in Figure 3.5.

SCM TP-1

```
0123456789:; = ?@ABCDEFGHIJKLMNOPQRSTUVWXYZ[  ]_@abcdefghijklmnopqrstuvw
0123456789:; = ?@ABCDEFGHIJKLMNOPQRSTUVWXYZ[  ]_@abcdefghijklmnopqrstuvw
0123456789:; = ?@ABCDEFGHIJKLMNOPQRSTUVWXYZ[  ]_@abcdefghijklmnopqrstuvw
```

Microline 92

```
Ø123456789:; <=) ?@ABCDEFGHIJKLMNOPQRSTUVWXYZ[\]^_@abcdefghijklmnopqrstuvw
Ø123456789:; <=) ?@ABCDEFGHIJKLMNOPQRSTUVWXYZ[\]^_@abcdefghijklmnopqrstuvw
Ø123456789:; <=) ?@ABCDEFGHIJKLMNOPQRSTUVWXYZ[\]^_@abcdefghijklmnopqrstuvw
```

Daisywriter 2000

```
 !"#$%&'()*+,-./0123456789:;<=>?@ABCDEFGHIJKLMNOPQRSTUVWXYZ[±]²_°abcdefghijklmno
pqrstuvwxyz¼½¶§!"#$%&'()*+,-./0123456789:;<=>?@ABCDEFGHIJKLMNOPQRSTUVWXYZ[±]²_°
abcdefghijklmnopqrstuvwxyz¼½¶§!"#$%&'()*+,-./0123456789:;<=>?@ABCDEFGHIJKLMNOPQ
```

FIGURE 3.5 A sample of output from three different printers.

Speed

Printer speeds vary from more than 200 characters per second to fewer than ten. If you are buying a printer for commercial use, a good high-speed printer will be important. For home use, a slower and less expensive printer usually is suitable.

Paper Size, Feed, and Movement

For various purposes, printers may be required to handle paper of different widths, continuous forms, multi-copy paper, envelopes, labels, etc. Decide what you need before you go on your printer quest. A standard size sheet of typing paper is $8\frac{1}{2}'' \times 11''$. Printers handle paper widths ranging from $2''$ to $16''$ or more. Fast becoming the standard for personal computers is continuous feed paper measuring $9\frac{1}{2}'' \times 11''$ with $\frac{1}{2}''$ punched strips on each side. Continuous feed means that the sheets are attached to each other by perforated seams. When the sheets of paper are torn apart and the strips are torn off the sides after printing, each sheet is the standard $8\frac{1}{2}'' \times 11''$.

There are two types of feed mechanisms — friction and tractor. A friction feed printer pulls the paper through the printer by means of pressure against the paper and the roller, much as a typewriter does. When continuous form paper is used in a friction feed printer, uneven paper feed can result, leading to binding and jamming of the paper. (For single sheets, friction feed works great.) Tractor feed mechanisms have little sprockets located on each side of the paper which engage a series of holes in the edge of the paper and pull it through the printer. This system works great for continuous feed paper. Some printers come with both tractor and friction feed capabilities.

Noise

Printers tend to be rather noisy creatures. Listen to the printer operate before you buy it and ask yourself if the noise it makes will be a problem in the environment where it will be used.

Interfaces

In order for your printer to receive information from your Apple, it must have what is known as an "interface." Most printers use either a "parallel" or "serial" interface. Some can use either. Your computer must have an interface of the correct type and a printer cable to connect the printer to the computer. There are several types of parallel and serial interfaces in general use. You can purchase just about any type of interface you need to work with the printer of your choice.

Cost and quality

Just as typewriters run the gamut from cheap home units to top quality office models, so do printers. If you are considering using your printer for business letters, a good letter quality printer would be a wise choice. This type of printer will range in cost from around $400 to several thousand dollars. These units are more expensive than the dot matrix units but provide better quality. If you anticipate less formal uses for your printer and desire the flexibility of having various print sizes and styles available or the ability to print graphics, then dot matrix printers are probably your cup of tea. Dot matrix printers range in price from less than $300 to about $2,000. Decide what you need and how much you can afford to spend before you go shopping.

Here's a representative sample of printers suited for use with the Apple.

Smith-Corona TP-2

At a list price of less than $700, this unit is often discounted to less than $600. The TP-2 is a friction feed, daisy wheel printer that comes with both parallel and serial interfaces. A tractor feed for the TP-2 is $150. The SCM TP-2 is one of the least expensive daisy wheel printers currently on the market. On the negative side, the T-2 is very noisy and slow. Its 18 characters per second rate is still a lot faster than most of us can type, but it is slow compared to other more expensive printers. On the positive side, the print quality is great. For good quality correspondence or printing where speed and noise are not primary factors, the TP-2 is a good choice. The TP-2 is carried in many local computer stores, and like most of the units, can also be ordered by mail.

Daisywriter 2000

If you want letter quality and can afford it, the Daisywriter 2000 is a good choice. It is relatively fast, fairly quiet and relatively smart. It includes a 16K buffer. (A buffer will allow you to use your computer for something else while your printer is at work.) The 2000 is a daisy wheel printer with both friction and tractor feed features, and both serial and parallel interfaces. The print quality is excellent. The list price is $1,395. This price is "deep discounted" in many areas. Some computer stores will carry the Daisywriter 2000 but it is not as popular as the SCM TP-2. It also can be ordered by mail.

Okidata ML 92

Okidata Corporation makes a line of good quality dot matrix printers suitable for use with the Apple. The ML-92 retails for $699. It is capable of very good "correspondence quality" print in several sizes and styles. It also can reproduce graphics and is fast — 160 characters per second. The nine-pin dot matrix head prints "descenders" — those parts of some letters which should descend below the normal bottom line of the letters like the y and g. Some printers do not have this capability. The appearance of their print, therefore, is not as good as those that do print descenders. Okidata printers use standard typewriter ribbons instead of the specially designed ribbon cartridges that most printers require. These are cheaper and more readily available than the ribbon cartridges. Okidata printers are carried by many local computer stores and are available from mail-order sources.

Okidata 2350

The 2350 is very similar to the ML-92, with the addition of the capability of two-color printing. Color printing is a rarity in the current crop of printers. This extra feature will cost you a little more, of course.

Epson RX-80 and FX-80

The Epson MX-80 became an historical landmark in the small computer industry after its introduction in 1979. It is still one of the most popular small printers. The updated versions of the MX-80 are the RX-80 and FX-80. The FX-80 includes graphics capability and costs about $100 more than the $300 RX-80. These are 9-pin dot matrix, tractor/friction feed printers. These printers have gained widespread acceptance because of their price, quality, and dependability. The Epson printers are a little slower than the Microline printers previously described. Epson printers use special ribbon cartridges which cost between $6 and $10 each. These are easier to install than standard typewriter ribbons, but they are more expensive and may be harder to find. Epson printers are widely available in computer stores, so supplies and repair service are more readily available than may be the case with some other printers. The 80 in the RX-, FX-, and MX-80 stands for 80 columns, which means that they can print up to 80 characters per line of 10 pitch type on 8½" wide paper. (Pitch relates to the size of the print. Ten pitch type is that most commonly used by typewriters and printers.) Other Epson printers have wider carriages to accept wider paper.

Com-Star f/t

This unit is a no-frills but inexpensive 80-column dot matrix printer. For under $300 you get seven-pin quality (no descenders) print at a relatively slow speed (for dot matrix printers) of 80 characters per second. The Com-Star f/t is capable of printing only three sizes of print and no graphics. This unit is not carried by many computer stores. It may be ordered directly from Protecto Enterprises. Local service will not be available, so you will have to ship it back to the factory when it needs repair. It uses a special ribbon cartridge, which also must be special ordered.

The Apple Printer Family

FIGURE 3.6 Three Apple printers. (Top) Letter quality, (bottom left) dot matrix, and (bottom right) Silentype printers.

Apple Computer distributes three printers for its computers. All are finished in Apple beige so you will not have to endure a printer whose color clashes with your Apple computer. These units, because of Apple policy, are not available by mail order in most instances, but are carried by many Apple dealers. Backed by the solid reputation of Apple, these units are all highly dependable. Service and supplies for them should be readily available. Because these units are designed to work with the Apple, the electronics are compatible. Another nice extra you get with Apple printers is a self-teaching disk so that your computer can teach you how to use your printer. A chief disadvantage of these units is their high cost compared to other printers.

The Silentype II. The main positive feature of this unit is its quietness. The Silentype is a thermal dot matrix printer. It uses a roll of specially treated paper to print characters by means of heating elements instead of pins that strike the paper through a carbon ribbon. The print quality is not good. The tan paper tends to curl up and, because it is heat sensitive, it can be ruined by exposure to extremes of heat. Don't leave an important program listing printed on the Silentype on the dashboard of your car in the summer or you will likely find a blackened mess when you return. The list price is $395 and that's not likely to be discounted much. Because no ribbon is used, you won't have that expense, but the specially treated thermal paper rolls can be a major expense. The Silentype II is not a very good buy unless you must operate your printer where quiet is the primary consideration.

The Apple Dot Matrix Printer. The Apple dot matrix printer is capable of producing five different type sizes and five different character sets. It also can give you proportional spacing, boldface, underlining, varied pitches, and varied line spacing. Graphics capability is built in, so it can produce neat, high-resolution graphics, such as charts and digitized portraits. The list price is $695, which is high compared to other similar printers.

The Apple Letter Quality Printer. This machine won't do graphics, but it is a speedy (40 characters per second), high-quality daisy wheel printer. The list price on this unit is $2,195. Varied sizes of print and spacing are possible. An adjustable tractor feed mechanism and friction control are included.

ADDING MEMORY TO YOUR APPLE

The size and complexity of programs which can be used and the amount of data which your Apple can handle is determined by the amount of RAM available. The Apple comes with a standard built-in RAM. Standard with the IIe is 64K. 48K was the standard in the II+ and II for several years. K, or kilobyte, stands for 1,024 bytes. Early Apples were sold with as little as 16K of memory. Many programs require at least 48K to operate. The disk operating system takes up some of this space, so you don't really have the full RAM capacity of your computer available for programs. A good rule of thumb regarding memories is that you never have enough.

A benchmark which can be used to give memory capacity a familiar meaning is the typed page. A letter-size page is 8½″ × by 11″. Such a

FIGURE 3.7 A RAM board.

page, typed and double spaced, has about 27 lines that are about 64 characters wide. This adds up to about 1,728 characters, including spaces, per page. One such page will require about 1.7K of memory. If you are planning to use your Apple for word processing, you will need at least enough memory to store several pages as well as space for the word processing program itself, which may require several K. Sixteen K would therefore be a bare minimum for word processing. At least 48K is preferred.

Fortunately, RAM expansion units are available which allow you to add memory capacity to the II and II+. Apple computer makes a 16K add-on memory card, sometimes called a language card because it can be used to store various computer languages. Other makes and models of RAM cards (language cards, memory expansion cards, add-on memory, for example) also are available from other manufacturers. The 16K RAM cards often are priced between $60 and $100. One 16K card has been nationally advertised for less than $45. Add-on memory tends to get proportionately more expensive after the first 16K. RAM boards made by Saturn are available in capacities of up to 128K and cost from about $240 for 32K to $600 for 128K. Prices for add-on memory have dropped dramatically in the past few years, and we can expect this trend to continue. The II+ can use up to 64K of RAM in normal operation; the IIe can use 128K with some programs.

GAME PADDLE CONTROLLERS

A wide range of game controllers, usually called paddles, are available for your Apple. These are necessary for playing most of the neat games discussed later in this book. Paddles come in a variety of shapes with many different features. Prices vary widely. So does reliability. Cost, construction, and personal preferences will determine which is best for you.

Early Apples came with set of cheap, flimsy paddles which had knobs and firing buttons that were too small. Over the years, the design has changed. The paddles currently sold by Apple no longer come with the computer when you purchase it, but may be ordered separately.

The Apple Hand Controller

The Apple hand controller sells for about $50 and is obviously designed for hand-held use. The firing button is on the right side and is large and flat so that it is easy to press. The knob is a two-tier design so that players may choose between large and small diameters. A "0" or "1" is thoughtfully molded on the center of each paddle knob so that you can readily distinguish between them. The paddles appear to be fairly sturdy, although we have found that these particular paddles develop problems after blasting space creatures for many hours.

Adam and Eve Paddles

These paddles have an attractive tapered shape which feels comfortable in the hand. The firing button is located on the left rear which seems to be the most preferred location for both right- and left-handed players. They produce a positive click when pressed as well as provide tactile feedback. Paddles 1 and 0 are labeled Adam and Eve respectively. The knob is about one inch in diameter, which seems to be about the right size for most users. An unusual feature of these units is an adjustable "trimmer" control which allows the paddle control knob rotation to be matched precisely to your computer or game. The trimmer also can be used to compensate for excessive wear. Five foot cables are included. A strain relief is included where the cables enter both the paddle housing and the computer. In summary, the Adam and Eve paddles are excellent, and at about $30, are very reasonably priced.

Joysticks

Joysticks, an alternative to paddles, combine the function of both paddle knobs into a single unit. In some games, these will give you greater control. For example, a game in which you move an airplane or space ship around

FIGURE 3.8 A joystick.

the screen might use one paddle to move the aircraft vertically and the other paddle for horizontal motion. This sort of game would be difficult to play with paddles because of the constant switching from one paddle to the other to control your craft. A joystick is the answer. (Maybe that's why many real airplanes use them.) There are many models of joysticks available for the Apple.

SPEECH SYNTHESIZERS

Talk is getting cheaper — at least for the Apple. Several devices are now available which allow you and your Apple to literally talk to each other. Devices which allow the computer to produce speech are called speech synthesizers. Devices which enable the computer to recognize your words are speech recognition units.

Speech recognition units are expensive and not highly reliable. The infinite variety of words, voice inflections, and possible pronunciations, gives speech recognition units fits. Improvements in this area can be expected in the next few years. For now most units are more novelty items than anything else.

The technology of speech synthesis is much more advanced than that of speech recognition. Most people say synthesized speech sounds mechanical or robot-like, but the words are recognizable and the vocabulary available is getting larger all the time. These units often have built-in speakers and electronic components that can transform words typed on the keyboard into verbal form. These units are useful in many applications. For example, children learning spelling words could hear the words pronounced by the computer and then spell them aloud or type them on the computer. Talking Apples also could add much excitement to games, and can add interest in almost any area.

The Echo GP

The Echo Speech Synthesizer from Street Electronics is sophisticated and fun to use. It connects to the computer as if it were a printer. When it is turned on, it responds with the phrase "Echo ready." You can use the built-in speaker of the unit or use a headphone. Several programs are available which use the Echo. One is the "textalker." This program is used with the Echo to convert English text into speech. With it, you could add speech to your BASIC programs by simply typing out the words or phrases desired. Echo has a rather unique accent and has trouble with "g" and "l" sounds, but unlike most other speech synthesizers it does not speak in a monotone. The list price of the unit is $300.

SAM

Software Automatic Mouth, SAM for short, is a combination software and hardware package which lists for $130 from Don't Ask Software. It combines an almost unlimited vocabulary with good intelligibility in an inexpensive unit. Connections are no more complicated than hooking up your Apple to a TV set. SAM can translate English text into speech which is only slightly inferior to the Echo. SAM comes with several demonstration programs, including a number of guessing games and some demo speeches. It is easy to work with from BASIC so that you can include speech in the programs you write. The instruction manual that comes with the unit is excellent.

Software Only Speech Synthesizers

The history of talking Apples goes back to 1979 when Softape Company released a program called Appletalker. This program is no longer sold, but many copies of it are still around. With it, your Apple can produce recognizable speech sounds through its built-in speaker with no additional hardware. The vocabulary available and speech quality of this program were not very good, but it was cheap and lots of fun anyway. Micro Users Software Exchange (MUSE) publishes an inexpensive program called the VOICE that serves the same purpose as Appletalker. If you would like to experiment with synthesized speech without spending a lot of money, this program is a good bet.

KEEPING TIME WITH YOUR APPLE

You can teach your Apple to tell time with the addition of a "clock." Apple clocks don't look like wristwatches, however. The clock is simply an accessory car with a minor addition — a nine-volt battery — that plugs into one of the Apple's accessory slots. The battery is needed to supply power when the Apple is turned off. There are no clock hands or digital readouts on Apple clocks. Their purpose is to time programs or provide time and date input or output for use in various programs. This can be a useful function in many programs. All large computers have electronic clocks so that the date and time can be added to printed reports or recorded when material is added to a file on the computer. Clocks also can save you the trouble of typing in date and time information in the many programs that need it.

Appletime Clock

The Appletime Clock system by Mountain Computer includes a datebook program to help you remember your appointments and provides time of day, calendar date, day of week, international time-keeping capability, and a rechargeable battery for a list price of $99. A software disk is included.

Thunderclock Plus

This unit is similar to, but more sophisticated than, Appletime Clock. The unit is made by Thunderware Products and sells for about $150. It is compatible with most major programs and can do any number of tasks for you automatically — such as store the date and time on your disk catalog each time a program is saved. With the addition of an optional interface, it can even turn on lights, water your lawn or whatever you desire at predesignated times.

ENHANCING THE TEXT SCREEN

Because the Apple II and II+ come with the capability to produce only capital letters in the video text display, one of the most popular and inexpensive accessories is a lowercase adapter. These little chips plug into the main circuit board and can be purchased for less than $30 from a variety of suppliers. With one of these in place, your basic Apple can print neat uppercase and lowercase letters on the screen. The IIe comes with built-in lowercase capability.

Because a standard piece of typing paper has space for 80 horizontal characters per line, most of us are accustomed to looking at text displayed in this manner. The II and II+ display only 40 characters per line on your TV screen. Eighty-column cards remedy this. The IIe often is sold with an Apple 80-column card that is made for it. The board also can be purchased separately.

At least eight manufacturers make 80-column boards (cards) for the II+ and II which range in price from $150 to almost $400. An 80-column display is important for many business applications and is almost a necessity for word processing. All 80-column boards are not alike. Some can be turned off to allow 40-column display. Some can't. Some allow you to use the shift key for capitals like a standard typewriter. Some use the escape key or another non-standard means of capitalization. Some boards will not work with the PASCAL language. Perhaps most importantly, some boards produce better looking characters than others. Our choice is the Viewmax-80 by Micromax. This unit is priced at less than $250, is PASCAL compatible, uses the shift key for capitalization, and forms attractive and professional looking text.

MODEMS TO COMMUNICATE WITH THE OUTSIDE WORLD

Modem is short for modulator-demodulator. Modems allow your Apple to communicate with other computers via telephone lines. As you type on the Apple's keyboard, the information being entered is converted to a modulated tone by the modem. This tone is then sent over telephone lines to another modem which is connected to another computer. The modem also will receive information sent to your Apple from other computers. Modems can be used to transfer just about any type of computerized information between two computers. They also can allow you to operate devices, such as printers and disk drives, attached to a distant computer. The addition of a modem could allow you to send and receive programs with other Apple users. In addition, you might wish to print out letters and reports compiled on your Apple on a letter quality printer in your college or business computer center. Modems also can allow you to use your Apple as a terminal for a larger computer. Using your Apple as a remote terminal can allow you to work on a large computer system from your home or office. With a modem, you also can gain access to any of several large networks of information available on a subscription basis, such as The Source or the CompuServe systems. This ability to communicate with the outside world opens many new doors for the Apple user. It is no wonder that modems are one of the most popular accessories for small computer users.

One of the main characteristics of modems is the speed at which they are capable of sending and receiving data — called the baud rate. A common rate of speed in modems used with microcomputers is 300 baud. A modem with a lower baud rate will be less expensive than one with a faster baud rate. A modem with a higher baud rate — say 1,200 — will transfer information faster, but will cost more. If you plan to connect your Apple to another computer in a distant city, the long distance charges will be higher with slower modems since it takes them longer to transfer and receive information.

Like all computer hardware, modems have been getting cheaper, faster, and better in recent years and the trend is likely to continue.

Here's a look at some of the more popular modems available for the Apple.

The Rixon PC 300

FIGURE 3.9 The Rixon PC modem.

This is a 300-baud modem in an attractive, streamlined case. The front panel has a neat row of little red LED lights and buttons to push. (Computer freaks love lights and buttons.) It sells for less than $160 and is manufactured by Rixon Inc. It comes with a cord and miniplug to connect it to a standard telephone jack. No telephone is needed. You also will need a serial interface (like those discussed in the earlier section on printers) to connect it to your Apple. The 300-baud speed is slow as modems go, but it is probably just fine for most small computer owners. For about $500, you can get the 1200-baud model.

The Apple Cat II

The Apple Cat II, by Novation, is a very popular little device that sells for $300 to $350. It is also a 300-baud unit with built-in interface. In addition to touchtone dialing capability, it has an auto dial/answer capabillity and a one year warranty. It plugs directly into the Apple through one of the expansion slots.

The SSM Apple Modemcard

This unit is probably indicative of the future of modems. It is contained entirely on a card which fits completely inside the Apple and plugs directly into one of the accessory slots. No telephone is required. It connects directly to the telephone jack and needs no separate interface. It is a 300-baud unit with several special features and has a two-year warranty. At less than $300, the SSM Apple Modemcard is a good choice.

EXPANDING YOUR BUSINESS SOFTWARE OPTIONS WITH CP/M AND Z80

This chapter would not be complete without the mention of one more important accessory — the Z80 card. The two most common microprocessors used in microcomputers are the 6502, on which the Apple is based, and the Z80, which is used in many other small computers. Many business programs use an operating system called CP/M, short for Control Program for Microcomputers. CP/M has become a defacto standard in the business world. More business programs have been written to work with this system than any other. This means that many business programs are not available to Apple users — unless you add a Z80 card.

A Z80 card contains a Z80 microprocessor and the CP/M operating system is usually provided on disk. The card plugs into one of the accessory slots on your Apple. Having an Apple with a Z80 card is like having two computers in one because it opens the door to a world of business programs not otherwise available to Apple users. For those who are interested in using the Apple for sophisticated business applications, this is well worth considering.

Several manufacturers make Z80 cards for the Apple. They are much alike and cost from $200 to $300. One popular Z80 card is the Z card from Advanced Logic Systems. This card retails for $269. For an extra fee, several popular CP/M-based business programs, such as the WordStar word processing program and Super Calc business spreadsheet program, can be purchased from the same source. Microsoft's Z80 card for the Apple is another of the more popular ones.

SUMMING IT UP

Many ways to enhance the capabilities of your basic Apple computer have been covered here. There are many other more specialized accessories which were not mentioned, and there are new devices coming into the market every month. To make the best choices, first decide on your computing priorities, then read up on your alternatives, and finally, comparison shop for price, support, and features for the devices you need. Most importantly, see the product demonstrated and ask questions. Manufacturers often make unsupported claims for their products. Check everything out thoroughly before you buy.

LIST OF PRODUCTS DISCUSSED IN CHAPTER 3

PRODUCT	**MANUFACTURER**
Apple Cat II	Novation Inc. 18664 Oxnard Tarzana, CA 91356
Rixon PC 300 Modem	Rixon Inc. 2120 Industrial Pky. Silver Spring, MD 20904
Viewmax-80 (80-column card)	JDR Microdevices 1224 Bascom Ave. San Jose, CA 95128
Dan Palmer LCA-1 & 2 (lowercase chips)	Dan Palmer 91 Pioneer Place Durango, CO 95128
Thunderclock Plus	Thunderware 44 Hermosa Ave. Oakland, CA 94618
Appletime Clock	MBI Corp. 1019 8th St., Suite 200 Golden, CO 80401
SAM Speech Synthesizer	Don't Ask Software 2265 Westwood Blvd., Suite B-150 Los Angeles, CA 90064
Echo Speech Synthesizer	Street Electronics 1140 Mark Ave. Cupertino, CA 93013
Adam and Eve Paddles	West Side Electronics Box 636 Chatsworth, CA 91311
Saturn RAM Boards	Saturn Systems Box 8050 Ann Arbor, MI 48107

PRODUCT	ADDRESS
SSM Apple Modemcard	SSM Microcomputer Products 2190 Paragon Drive San Jose, CA 95131
Amdek Color Monitors	Amdek Corp. 2701 Lively Rd. Elk Grove Village, IL 60007
NEC Monitors	NEC Home Electronics 1401 Estes Ave. Elk Grove Village, IL 60007
Jade Monitors	Jade Computer Products 4901 W. Rosecrans Hawthorne, CA 90250
Zenith Monitors	Zenith Corporation 1000 Milwaukee Glenview, IL 60025
Guardian Angel Power Supply Superfan II	R & H Electronics 566 Irelan Buelton, CA 93427
Lemon Surge Protector	Electronic Protection Devices 5 Central Ave. Waltham, MA 02154
Cool Mark II Fan	Mark Four Imports Box A San Gabriel, CA 91776
System Saver Fan	Kensington Microfare 300 E. 54th St., Suite 3L New York, NY 10022
Micro Sci Disk Drives	Micro Sci Disk Drives 2158 S. Hathaway St. Santa Anna, CA 92705

PRODUCT	**ADDRESS**
Lobo Disk Drives	Lobo Drives 358 S. Fairway Ave., Dept A011 Goleta, CA 93177
Okidata Printers	Okidata Enterprises Mt. Laurel, NJ 08054
Com-Star Printers	Protecto Enterprises Box 550 Barrington, IL 60010
Smith-Corona TP-2 Printer	Smith-Corona 65 Locust Ave. New Canaan, CT 06840
Daisywriter 2000 Printer	Computers International 3540 Wilshire Blvd. Los Angeles, CA 90010
Epson Printers	Epson America Inc. 3415 Kashina St. Torrence, CA 90505
Z-Card	Advanced Logic Systems 1195 E. Arques Sunnyvale, CA 94086

Products by Apple Computer:

Silentype II Printer Apple Letter Quality Printer Apple Dot Matrix Printer Apple Hand Controller Apple Paddles Apple Disk II Drive Monitor III	Apple Computer Inc. 20525 Mariani Ave. Cupertino, CA 95014

Chapter 4

Maintaining Your Apple

*"I don't know what happened . . . it just sort of hiccupped! It was
running fine and then all of a sudden it started doing strange things. It
gronked . . . went off to never-never land."*

Apples are generally quite reliable, but every once in a while you hear
statements like the one above. Some preventive maintenance will reduce
the likelihood of disaster striking your Apple. When problems do occur,
it may be possible to correct them without hauling your Apple off to the
repair shop. Repair shops are often slow and almost always expensive.
This chapter offers conventional wisdom gained from several years of
debugging and caring for these mostly faithful computers. Care and minor
repairs are discussed for the Apple itself and for the most common accessories — disk drives, printers, and game controllers. The most common
types of problems associated with each device are reviewed and tips on
correcting these problems are given. All of the procedures described here
can be done with a few simple tools and no advanced training.

FINDING THE SOURCE OF THE PROBLEM

Many common problems can be caused by a variety of things — faulty
chips, loose connections, bad solder joints, etc. Often, fixing the computer
is not as much of a problem as finding out what's causing the problem in
the first place. Several programs are available that enable the user to test
the computer, the disk, and even the printer. These programs will be
discussed in Chapter 7. The IIe also comes with a built-in set of self-diag-
nostic routines.

The IIe Self-Diagnosis Procedure

The IIe has a set of built-in routines so you can test it whenever you like. Just press the **CONTROL**, **RESET**, and **CLOSED APPLE** keys (three keys at once), and the Apple will test the entire memory and display the results in high-resolution graphics. If any faulty chips are found, check them out with the following procedures and run the test again. New chips can be purchased from most computer vendors. You can easily replace them yourself with a chip insertion tool.

Most computer failures are caused by one or more common problems. We'll look briefly at each type of problem and some likely remedies.

CHIP PROBLEMS

Oxidation and dirt are the main causes of chip problems. Apple Computer does not solder the chips in its computers directly to the motherboard. Rather, Apple uses sockets so that chips can be inserted and removed easily. Chemicals and moisture in the air can gradually corrode chip leads. When oxidation builds up, something (or everything) will stop working. Chip leads can be cleaned with a cotton swab dipped in alcohol. If you suspect that you have a faulty chip, remove it carefully from the socket with a chip insertion/removal tool, clean each lead and reinsert it in the socket.

The constant heating and cooling caused by turning the computer off and on can cause the chips to work their way out of the sockets. To guard against loose chips, you should periodically press them back into their sockets. Perhaps once every six months, with the power off, place one hand on the power supply box to ground yourself and drain off any static electricity in your body. Then press gently on each chip with the other hand. Be careful not to push too hard or you may damage the circuit board.

There are cheap chips and expensive ones. One of the main factors in cost is the material used in manufacturing the leads. Better chips have gold-plated leads. These are more resistant to corrosion and make better contact with the socket. When you purchase accessories, this is a good point to check out.

Bent Pins

We once had an intermittent problem with an Apple. Whenever the memory chips were pushed a little to seat them better in their sockets, the problem went away. However, the problem got worse as time went on, so we decided to remove all the chips for cleaning and inspection. When about half the chips were out, one was found with a bent lead. It was completely bent up 180 degrees. It had come from the factory that way. Periodic pressing on it kept it working, but just barely. Straightening the pin with a pair of tweezers and reinserting the chips cured the problem. There are probably many Apples out there with this problem just waiting to bedevil their owners at the least convenient time.

It is easy to bend one of the little chip lead pins when inserting them, so when installing a new accessory or reinserting chips after cleaning, follow this procedure: Push the chip halfway into the socket and stop. Look carefully at all of the pins to see if they are entering the socket straight. If they are, push the chip completely into the socket.

CIRCUIT BOARD PROBLEMS

The main circuit board (motherboard) has many solder "traces" which connect the various components and chip sockets. Cracked or broken traces and poor solder connections can cause many types of intermittent problems. Rough handling can lead to warping which can cause circuit traces and solder joints to break (although this is rare). I have heard of some techno-freaks who solved problems of this type by taking their Apples apart and touching up all the solder joints with a soldering iron. I do not recommend this unless you are experienced with electronics, but if you must try it, be sure to remove all the chips first. The heat from soldering can ruin them. Store chips in a piece of conductive foam material or a packing tube for protection while they are out of the computer.

Heat Problems

If your Apple overheats, you are asking for trouble. Excessive heat will cause premature failure in many components. Loose or damaged chips may cause freaky intermittent problems. Keep the slots on the sides of your Apple clear of obstructions so that air can circulate freely. If you have a II or II+ with three or more accessory cards or a IIe with four or more cards, buy a fan like one of those described in Chapter 3.

Static Electricity

Static electricity is an enemy of all computers. If you touch the disk drive while it is on after your body builds up a good static charge from walking on your carpet, it can go through the disk case to the read/write head, zapping your disk. It can even travel inside the computer causing all sorts of problems. One static charge can be enough to wipe out a chip.

Static electricity can be minimized by using anti-static carpet. Anti-static carpet sprays also help. Anti-static sprays can be purchased from computer stores, but you can make your own by mixing fabric softener with water in a 1:4 ratio. Apply the solution with a spray bottle to the carpet in the room where the computer is located. Extremely dry climates and low humidity frequently found in homes and offices during the winter make static electricity worse. This can be helped by use of a humidifier.

Your Apple should always be grounded properly. Never plug your computer into an ungrounded electrical outlet (one with two holes instead of three) without attaching a ground wire. If you must use your Apple in an old building that does not have grounded outlets, connect the ground wire from the adapter to a water pipe or rod stuck into the ground. Grounding not only helps with static electricity, but also is a primary safety feature to guard against shock, fire, and damage to electrical appliances which can be caused by short circuits.

Magnetic Fields

Magnetic fields (or flux) caused by electric motors, welders, furnaces, and other electric devices can erase your disks if the field is strong enough. When the air conditioner failed on a hot day, we once carelessly placed an electric fan on a computer station. Problems began to crop up with saving and loading programs. When the fan was removed, the problem went away.

Some TVs, especially older models, generate a considerable magnetic field. Vacuum cleaners also can be bad news for computers. Keep running vacuum cleaners at least four feet away from your disks. One way to check for magnetic flux is to use the telephone. Press one number on the dial to kill the dial tone, and move the phone receiver around the computer. If you hear a buzz, there is a strong magnetic field present.

MAINTAINING THE DISK DRIVE

Disk drive units are generally highly reliable, but, like all other mechanical devices with moving parts, they are subject to some problems. Disks that fail to boot, programs that once loaded but later refuse to, or I/O ERROR messages after an attempt to save a program are common indicators of disk drive problems. Some of the common causes of problems and guidelines for preventing them are discussed here.

Disk Speed

The Apple Disk II Drive operates at a speed of 300 rpm (rotations per minute). If this speed is not fairly accurate, your disk drive will not be able to find the beginning and end of the tracks on which your programs are stored on the disk. Variations of ±10 rpm can cause errors. Attempts to load programs from a disk drive that is operating too slowly or too fast will fail. Attempts to save programs on a disk that is operating at the wrong speed may appear to work correctly, but may actually write over previously stored programs, resulting in permanent loss of all or part of the programs on the disk. Programs to check the speed of the disk drive are available from several sources. One such program is Apple-Cillin, which is discussed in Chapter 7.

Cleaning the Read/Write Head

Disk drives use a tiny electromagnetic head which comes in contact with the disk to read and write information to and from the disk. Over time, the friction caused by the spinning disk will cause residue from the emulsion on the disk surface to build up on the head. Eventually, this will get bad enough to cause problems with loading and saving operations. These problems can be prevented by regular cleaning of the head.

Heads do not need to be cleaned nearly as often as the manufacturers of head-cleaning kits would like us to believe. Advertisements frequently state that heads should be cleaned every time you use your computer. Once every few months is probably often enough to clean the heads, if you give your drives pretty regular use. Even if you use them frequently every day, a cleaning every month usually should be adequate. Excessive cleaning of the head can cause more problems than it fixes. The easiest way to clean the head of a disk drive is with a cleaning kit that you'll find at most computer stores. These use little fabric disks to which you apply a few drops of cleaner. They save you the trouble of taking the drive apart to clean the head.

Pressure Pad Replacement

The Apple Disk II drive uses a little felt-tipped pressure pad (located directly opposite the read/write head) to press the disk firmly against the head and ensure good contact. The friction caused by the spinning disk against the pad will eventually cause oxide residue to build up on the pad. You can tell when this has become bad enough to cause problems because your drive will begin to sing with a high-pitched squeal when the drive is on. It is possible to obtain a replacement pad from your Apple dealer and replace it yourself, but for most people this is a bit involved given that it calls for removal of the disk drive's circuit board. We recommend that you let the repair shop do this.

Closing the Door — Easy Does It

One final tip on disk drives — don't slam the little door after inserting a disk. Doing so can cause crimping of the center hole of the disk. This is permanent damage. When it happens, the disk may start to give I/O errors. Better disks have a plastic reinforcing hub ring around the center hole that helps prevent this from happening. But even if your disks have hub rings, you should close the drive door gently.

MAINTAINING PRINTERS

Because of the great diversity in the various makes and models of printers, only common problems and general maintenance procedures will be discussed here. Consult the owner's manual that accompanies your printer for more information.

Cleaning

Paper moving through the printer gradually will cause some paper dust residue to build up inside the unit. Dust will accumulate from the air also. Ink from the ribbon will produce some residue on the guide posts and other parts it contacts. To prevent sticking or jamming from all of this, it's a good idea to clean your printer regularly. To determine whether cleaning is needed, remove your printer's cover and look inside. If you see a significant amount of dust and debris, it's time to clean house. Wiping off the parts with a soft cloth will help. A vacuum cleaner with a furniture nozzle attachment may be necessary to get all the dust from hard to reach places. (Don't get the vacuum cleaner too close to your disks.) Typewriter cleaner applied with cotton swabs or a soft cloth may be useful to clean gunk from the moving parts or the rubber rollers on your printer.

Print-Too-Light Problems

Get a new ribbon when the print starts getting light. The owner's manual with the printer will tell you what type you need and how to install it. Keep several on hand so you'll have one when you need it. You can rejuvenate old ribbons by spraying a little WD-40 oil on them and letting them stand overnight. To do this with cartridge ribbons it will be necessary to remove the top of the catridge. Note that we said a little oil! Don't overdo it.

If a new ribbon doesn't produce crisp, neat print, you may need to adjust the pressure of the print head against the paper. Most printers will have a means to do this. Usually an adjustment screw or lever is provided near the ends of the print roller. Multiple form paper will require greater pressure.

Too much pressure will cause the print head to drag the ribbon against the paper and leave a streak or smear.

Paper Alignment Problems

Paper is moved through the printer by either friction or tractor feed which was discussed in Chapter 3. Printers with friction feed capability will have a friction release lever, usually located at the rear right of the roller. Release the friction to insert and align your paper as you do on a typewriter, but don't forget to put the pressure back on before operating your printer.

Tractor feed printers use sprocket wheels to engage holes in the edges of the paper to pull it through the printer. The sprocket wheel placement probably will be adjustable to accommodate different paper widths. Usually, levers adjacent to the sprocket wheels can be released so they can be moved. If these are not positioned properly when loading paper, torn sprocket holes and jammed or torn paper can result. If you are using a printer with both friction and tractor feed mechanisms, release the friction control when you are using continuous form paper with tractor feed. Having the friction feed pressure on while using the tractor feed is unnecessary and may cause crimping and jamming of the paper.

GAME PADDLE PROBLEMS

Once Bob took a set of paddles that had stopped functioning to a computer store for repair. He was told by the dealer that the minimum charge for any repair was $40. Because this is about the cost of a new set of paddles, he decided to have a crack at fixing them himself. He found that game paddles are pretty simple and can usually be repaired easily. The main problems seem to fall into these areas:

Broken Wires

Twisting or jerking on the paddles (perhaps in a fit of grief as your space ship is zapped by the alien invaders) can break the little wires inside the cables rendering the paddle useless. Most often this occurs at the point where the wires enter the paddle. If this is the case, the problem can be fixed by cutting the cable a couple of inches back from the paddle, removing the paddle cover and reconnecting the wires. Soldering may be necessary. If this doesn't fix the problem, you can keep repeating the procedure as long as the cable lasts. As a last resort, take a piece of the cable to Radio Shack and buy a new cable wire of the same type and replace the whole thing.

Wires also can break inside the paddle. To check for this, carefully remove the cover of the paddle and inspect all the connections. If you find a broken wire and can't tell for sure where it goes, remove the cover on the other paddle to check it out. You will probably have to resolder the connection.

Defective Rotary Control

The rotary control portion of the game controller is actually a variable resistor also correctly called a potentionmeter or rheostat. It is much the same as the volume control on a radio. These eventually will stop functioning after much twisting and turning. These devices are used in many electronic components. With a little luck and persistence, you may find a replacement at a local hi-fi shop or Radio Shack store. There are many different kinds of these in use, so take the old broken one with you on your search. Potentionmeters are measured in resistance values expressed in ohms. The nominal value expected by your Apple is 150k ohms. Anything between 70k ohms and 185k ohms should work if it will fit inside the paddle.

Defective Firing Button

The firing button on the game controller is just an open circuit switch. Contact is made, and the circuit completed, when the button is pressed. Faulty buttons either will not make good contact which will keep you from firing your phasers, or will be locked in the closed position which will make them fire all the time. Little buttons like this are readily available from Radio Shack or any other place that sells small electronic components and it should be no problem to find a replacement. Take the old one with you when you go to the store to make sure that you get one that will fit the paddle.

Most folks we know just stick the old paddles in a drawer and buy a new set. This is the easiest way out, but with a little patience, the do-it-yourselfer can fix most common paddle problems.

THE BOTTOM LINE

The Apple computer is a highly dependable device that will give you many hours of trouble free operation with a minimum of problems. Very little maintenance is required, but it will need some care to keep it running smoothly. The bottom line is that it is the owner's responsibility to see that this is done. Preventing problems by regular preventive maintenance is the best solution. If problems do develop, you can often save much time and money by doing a few simple repairs yourself.

Chapter 5

Quick and Dirty BASIC

HOW TO USE THIS CHAPTER

It's time to meet the popular computer language called BASIC. It is assumed that you have read Chapters 1 and 2 of this book, that you have made all connections properly, are familiar with the procedures for operating your Apple, and know how to save and load programs.

There are at least 200 books currently in print that teach you how to write programs in BASIC. There are at least 20 books that deal specifically with programming the Apple. We're not going to teach you to write complex programs. But after finishing this chapter, you should be able to write simple BASIC programs, understand a simple program listing written by someone else, make minor corrections and enhancements to programs, and have a good idea of where to go for more information on programming if you want it.

It probably is best to read this while sitting in front of the computer. Learn what the new terms mean by using your computer to do the examples provided. Don't try to memorize definitions. It is more important that you know where to find information than it is to be able to say off the top of your head what GOSUB 100 means. BASIC will become a familiar second language through experience, not memorization.

One of Apple's most popular publications is *The Applesoft BASIC Programming Reference Manual*. These were supplied with the Apple II + s and IIs at the time of purchase. They do not come with the IIe, but are available, in a three-volume set, from your Apple dealer. The *Reference Manual* is a thorough description of all the BASIC commands. The *Reference Manual* is thick and does not make for easy reading. However, we recommend that you buy it and keep it beside your Apple to consult whenever you need to look up something.

The programs contained in this book may be typed into the computer by the reader and may be saved for later use on a disk or tape. However, if you wish to save yourself the bother of typing them, a disk containing all programs included here, plus several bonus programs, may be ordered by sending $10.00 to Sunbelt Computing, 7807 Kenosha, Lubbock, TX 79423.

INTRODUCTION TO BASIC

BASIC, short for Beginners All-Purpose Symbolic Instruction Code, is currently the most popular programming language used in small computers. The Apple IIe and II+ come with a built-in version of BASIC called Applesoft. The II came with a slightly different version of BASIC called Integer BASIC. However, Applesoft BASIC can easily be added to the II. Only Applesoft BASIC will be covered here because this is the current, state-of-the-art version of the language spoken by the Apple IIe and II+.

BASIC, FORTRAN, and COBOL are languages of computers much as English, French, and Japanese are languages of people. There are several important differences between the languages spoken by computers and those spoken by people. One important difference is the limited vocabulary and rigidity of computer languages. In English there are usually several words with similar meanings which you might use to communicate your ideas. To describe a 1955 Chevrolet, you might use the words car, automobile, auto, or vehicle. English is a rich and forgiving language. Even if you misspelled a word, your messages would probably still be clear. Computer languages are not so forgiving. You must say what you mean exactly as the computer expects.

Another difference between computer languages and human languages is the way punctuation is handled. Commas, periods, and semicolons clarify the meanings of words in English, but rules for their use are somewhat flexible. You probably could understand a letter from a second grader even if it did not contain a single mark of punctuation. In BASIC, these punctuation marks are often just as important as the letters and numbers. Leaving one comma out can sometimes prevent an entire program from running properly.

The words BASIC understands are called "key words." These words are used to make "statements." Statements correspond to sentences in English. Here are three examples of statements:

```
10 A = 2
20 B = 4
30 PRINT A + B
RUN
```

Each statement is preceded by a line number. When a computer is told to **RUN** a program, it begins with the statement that has the lowest line number and follows the instructions given in that statement. It then proceeds through all the statements until all have been executed or **RUN**. When it reaches line 30 in the program, it will do the arithmetic and print the results on the screen. These three statements make up a simple program. Turn on your Apple, boot DOS if are using a disk drive, and type **NEW**. Now type this program on your Apple and **RUN** it. **The CAPS LOCK must be down if you are using the IIe.**

A program is a set of instructions which tell the computer what to do. Computers are incredibly dumb. They wake up in a whole new world each time they are turned on, having totally forgotten everything that they were "taught" by previous programs. Without programs, computers are as useless as a car without a steering wheel.

You normally tell a computer that you want it to execute a program (follow the instructions) by giving it the command, **RUN**. However, there is another way. If you type **PRINT** 4 + 2, the computer will print 6 immediately after you press **RETURN**. In this case, you do not have to type **RUN**. If you do not put a line number in front of a statement, the Apple assumes that you want the instructions carried out immediately. Therefore, this method of using the computer is often called the "immediate" mode. The same line typed with a line number (e.g., 10 **PRINT** 4 + 2) is recognized by the computer as part of a program. Execution of the instruction is deferred until the program is executed. Try it on your Apple.

Most of the key words in BASIC can be used either in the immediate mode or the deferred mode. If **PRINT** is used in a program, it is called a statement in most textbooks. A few key words, such as **RESUME**, **INPUT**, **GET**, and **RETURN**, can be used only in program statements while a few others, such as **RUN** and **LIST**, can be used effectively only as commands in the immediate mode.

PROGRAM CONTROL COMMANDS

Several of the key words used in BASIC are used to tell the computer how to manage its work. These are called program control commands. The most important of these are listed here with an explanation of what they do:

RUN. This command already has been used several times. When you give the **RUN** command, it tells the computer to execute the instructions contained in the program currently in the computer's memory. Normally, **RUN** tells the computer to begin with the instructions in the line with the lowest number. However, if you tell the Apple to **RUN** 70, it will start executing the instructions in line 70. Any line numbers less than 70 will not be executed. **RUN** also can be used with a program name. This will cause a program located on a disk to be both loaded and run as explained in Chapter 2.

NEW. This command clears the computer's RAM. Always type **NEW** before you begin typing a new program. If you don't, the computer will think that your new program is part of your old program. The results can be a mess. Any time that you want to start fresh, with nothing left of the old program, type **NEW**. Before you use **NEW**, be sure you really do want to erase everything in memory. Once it's done, it's done. **NEW** can be used effectively only as a command in the immediate mode.

CLEAR. Clear lets you erase values assigned to variables without erasing the program in memory. For example, if you have **RUN** the sample program given earlier which contained the line A = 5, A will still equal five after the program has finished running. If the program is still in your computer's memory, type **PRINT** A now. Your computer should respond with a 5. If you want to clear the memory of all variables (such as A), enter **CLEAR**. Now enter **PRINT** A again. Your Apple will respond with 0. The Apple will automatically assign all variables a value of 0 unless you tell it differently. **CLEAR** can be used either as a program statement or as a command in the immediate mode.

SAVE and LOAD. These commands were covered in Chapters 1 and 2. These commands used alone cause the computer to **LOAD** or **SAVE** programs on cassette tape. With the addition of a program name, these commands will cause the computer to use the disk drive. For example, **SAVE PRACTICE PROGRAM** will tell the computer to save the program currently in the computer's memory on the disk and name it PRACTICE PROGRAM. These commands are most often used in the immediate mode, but they also can be used as program statements.

LIST. This command tells the computer that you wish to see the lines of the current program displayed on the video display. **LIST** will cause the entire program to be listed. If it contains less than 25 lines, the entire program can be listed on the screen at once, given that your Apple displays 24 lines on the screen at the same time. If your program is longer than 24 lines, it will scroll off the top of the screen and leave only the last 24 lines displayed. To prevent this, you also can use **LIST** with line numbers. For example, **LIST** 50 would list only line 50. **LIST** 1,50 would list lines 1 through 50. **LIST** 50- would list all lines starting with line 50 through the end of the program. **LIST** generally can be used effectively only as a command in the immediate mode.

HOME. This command clears the screen and sends the cursor to the upper left-most position (its home). It can be used either as a command or a statement in a program.

CONTROL/C. Pressing the control key (marked **CTRL** on the II + and II and **CONTROL** on the IIe), together with the C key will cause a program that is being executed or listed to halt. **LOAD** and **RUN** any program from your system master or another disk. While the program is running, press **CONTROL/C**. The program will halt immediately and the cursor will reappear. Now **LIST** the program, and while the program is listing, press **CONTROL/C** again. The listing will immediately stop.

ESC/A, B, C, or D. These commands move the cursor around in the same manner as the arrow keys. **ESC/A** moves the cursor one space to the right. **ESC/B** moves it one space to the left. **ESC/C** moves it one space down, and **ESC/D** moves it one space up.

SPEED = X. By using the command **SPEED** together with a number between 1 and 255, you can slow down the speed at which your Apple runs or lists a program. For example, enter **SPEED** = 50. Now **RUN** your program. Notice things happen a lot slower than normal. Stop the program with a **CONTROL/C**. Now enter **SPEED** = 255. **RUN** your program again and things will be back to normal.

PR#6. This command is functionally equivalent to turning the Apple off and then on again. It clears the RAM and reinstalls the DOS. It can be used in either the immediate or deferred mode.

PR#1 and PR#0. PR#1 directs the Apple to send its output to the printer (if you have one). Programs that are **RUN** or listed after **PR#1** has been typed will be printed on paper. The output will be displayed on the video screen at the same time that the programs are printed. **PR#0** turns the printer off. These commands may be used either in the immediate or deferred mode.

EDITING PROGRAMS

Editing is useful to correct mistakes and to make changes in programs. Editing programs is simple and easy on the Apple. By deleting words or lines, and adding new ones, changes and corrections can be made efficiently. Editing procedures are the same on the II and II + . The editing procedures on the II + and II also will work exactly the same on the IIe. However, the IIe has some additional features which the II + and II do not have. First, let's look at the basic procedures common to all the IIs and then consider the additional features on the IIe separately.

Basic Editing Procedures

Correcting Mistakes Before a Line Has Been Entered. If you make an error while typing a line (before you enter it by pressing **RETURN**), you can correct your error by following this procedure:

1. Use the ← key to move the cursor back to the error. (II + and II users can make the cursor move rapidly along the line by holding the ←

key and **REPT** keys down at the same time. (Users of the IIe need only hold down the ← key.)

2. Once you have the cursor positioned over the mistake, simply type the correct character. The old character will be deleted as the new one is entered.

3. Now use the → key to return the cursor to the end of the line. This is very important. The → recopies any characters over which the cursor passes. If you don't recopy the rest of the line in this manner, only the part of the line to the left of the cursor will be entered into the computer's memory.

4. As always, press **RETURN** when your corrected statement is ready to be entered into the computer's memory.

To illustrate this procedure, let's assume that you have typed the following line:

100 PRINY "HELLO, I AM THE APPLE COMPUTER."

Before you enter the line, you notice that you have typed a Y instead of a T in **PRINT**. By pressing the ←, you can move the cursor until it is over the Y. Then press a T. The Y will disappear and the T will be substituted for it. Now press the → until the cursor is past the last character on the line. Finally, press **RETURN** to enter the line. Try this out on your Apple.

Editing a Line After It Has Been Entered. Once a line has been entered, you may correct it in one of two ways. One way is to retype the entire line. The Apple will delete the old line when a new one with the same line number is entered. To demonstrate this, enter the sample line 100 shown in the last example, mistake and all, on your Apple. Try to run it. What happens? You will see an error message that reads: SYNTAX ERROR IN 100. Now retype and enter the line correctly as shown here:

100 **PRINT** "HELLO, I AM THE APPLE COMPUTER."

List the program by typing and entering **LIST**. You will see line 100 listed as you last typed it. **RUN** the program. The computer will now understand what you want it to do and will obligingly print the sentence on the screen. Experiment with this procedure until you have it down pat.

An alternative to retyping the entire line is editing with the Apple's built-in editor. If you have a rather long statement with only a few mistakes in it, you can save typing time by correcting them in this manner:

1. Press the **ESCAPE** key once to enter the edit mode.

2. Move the cursor on the IIe with the arrow keys or use the I, J, K, or M keys on the II+ or II (I=up cursor, M=down cursor, K=right

cursor, J = left cursor). Once you have the cursor positioned at the point on the line where the change is needed, press any key other than I, J, K, or M (or an arrow key on the IIe) to exit from the cursor control mode.

3. Use the ← to back up all the way to the beginning of the line. This is very important.

4. Use the → key to move the cursor to the point where the change is needed.

5. Type the new word or words, and the old ones will be deleted as the new ones are typed.

6. When the change has been made, double check your typing, then move the cursor past the end of the line with the → key and press **RETURN**.

This will kill the old version of the line and enter the new one. To try out this procedure, enter **NEW** to clear out the old program and enter the sample program below exactly as it is shown:

```
10 TEXT:CLEAR:HOME
20 PRINT "NOW IT THE TIMR FOR ALL GOOD CITIZENS
   TO COME TO THE AID OF THERE COUNTRYY"
30 END
```

Line 20 has several mistakes in it. Rather than retype the entire line, you can save time by just replacing the wrong letters with the right ones. To do this, press **ESCAPE** once. Then move the cursor (with the arrow keys on the IIe or the I, J, K, and M keys on the II+ or II) as needed until it is located anywhere on line 20. Press the space bar to exit the cursor control mode. Before you can edit the line, the cursor first must be moved to a position over the 2 in 20. Move it to the 2 with the ← key. Now use the → key to move the cursor until it is located over the R in what should be TIME. Type an E. After this is done, press the → key several times until it is located over the R in THERE. Press an I and then an R. THERE will now read THEIR.

Press the right arrow key again until it is over the second Y in COUN-TRYY. Because we only need one Y, we can get rid of the extra one by killing it and moving the rest of the line over one place. So type the period (.) in place of the Y, followed by the end quote mark ("). Next, press the space bar to kill the extra quote. The extra Y was replaced by a period. The old period was replaced by a quote mark, and the old quote mark was replaced by a blank. Press **RETURN** and the corrected version of the line is entered into the computer.

The Apple computer will not allow you to insert new words in the middle of a statement. For example if you wished the line to read: NOW IS THE TIME FOR ALL GOOD AND ABLE CITIZENS TO COME TO THE

AID OF THEIR COUNTRY, you would have no choice except to retype the entire line in order to add the words "AND ABLE" to the statement.

Words can be deleted if they are not in the middle of a quote statement. For example, if we wished to delete the word GOOD entirely from the sentence, this would necessitate retyping the entire line. However, if we wished to delete the command **CLEAR** from line 10, this could be done by following the editing procedure previously described. Experiment with editing in this manner until you are accustomed to it.

Additional Editing Features Available on the Apple IIe

A major feature of the IIe is the addition of improved editing capabilities. The additional features are:
1. Visible prompt identifying edit mode.
2. Additional editing keys and features.
3. Restricted case mode.

Visible Prompt Editing. In normal operation, the cursor on the IIe is a small flashing checkerboard square. If you have the 80-column board (discussed in Chapter 2) installed on your IIe, invoking the 80-column mode with a PR#3 command will provide you with additional editing capabilities. First, the cursor will change to a solid white block which does not flash. When the **ESCAPE** key is pressed, the cursor becomes an inverse "+." This enables you to tell readily that the computer is in the cursor control mode for editing. You can tell easily from the cursor whether you are entering commands or editing. Once in the cursor control mode, the + cursor can be moved about the screen by using the arrow keys. (The I, J, K, and M keys also can be used to move the cursor on the IIe just as on the II+ and II for long-time Apple users who just can't break old habits.)

Restricted Case Mode. One of the primary improvement of the IIe over the II+ is its ability to display lowercase letters. However, the Applesoft programming language will accept only uppercase letters. If you type the line 10 Print "Hello" on your IIe, you will receive a SYNTAX ERROR message when the program is **RUN**. Applesoft doesn't understand "Print." It only understands "**PRINT**."

There is a solution to this dilemma. The IIe's answer is the "restricted case mode." Pressing **ESCAPE/R** will initiate this. In the restricted case mode, all letters are forced into uppercase by the computer regardless of whether or not you capitalize, until a quote (") is encountered. Then lowercase is accepted until another quote is encountered. To demonstrate this, type **NEW** to clear your Apple's memory and then press **ESCAPE/R**.

Now type the following line using the shift key to form capitals as you normally would on a typewriter.

>   100 HOME:"PRINT "This is a demonstration of the restricted
>   case mode."

When we first tried this technique, it seemed awkward, but soon we realized that forcing the computer to keep track of where capitals are required is a deft solution to the uppercase/lowercase problem. Use **ESCAPE/T** to turn off the restricted case mode. Experiment with this on your IIe until you feel comfortable with it.

BEGINNING APPLESOFT

If you are just sitting down at the computer, turn on the computer and the TV or monitor, and boot DOS. If you are using Applesoft BASIC, the square bracket prompt character (]) will appear to the left of the cursor on the screen. This means that the computer is ready to receive your program in Applesoft BASIC. (Different languages have different prompts.)

Variables

Variables are actually labels or names of values. Your name and age could be variables. If your name is Bob and your age is 35, Bob and 35 are the values of the variables NAME and AGE. Computers use variables extensively to allow storage and manipulation of information. We'll look at how computers use variables shortly in some practice programs.

There are two basic kinds of variables — numeric, such as age, and alphabetic, such as names. Variables which are comprised partly or entirely of alphabetic characters are called "strings" and are represented by the dollar sign ($) when writing programs. If we wanted to store the program user's name in a variable, we might call the variable NAME$. You can name variables almost anything you wish. Names could be stored in variables X$, Y$, N$, NAM$, or just about anything else you can think of, as long as the dollar sign ($) is placed at the end. However, we suggest that meaningful variable names be used. It is much easier to understand a program listing which uses NAME$ than one that uses X$ to store a name.

The Apple recognizes only the first two characters of a variable name as significant. In other words, it reads only the first two characters. The variable NAME$ is seen by the Apple as NA$. This means that you must take care when writing programs to use the first two-letter combination in any variable name only once in any program. If you name one variable MONTH$ and another MONEY$, the Apple will get the two variables mixed up because they both start with MO. To avoid confusion, it is a good idea to a make a list of all the variables used in a program as you write it. This way you can easily check your "variable table" to see which names or labels have been used.

Notice that we said you can name variables "almost" anything you wish. You may not use Applesoft key words as variable names. For example, the commands listed earlier in this chapter, such as **LIST**, **NEW**, **PRINT**, **LOAD**, etc. cannot be used as variable names. Because the Apple recognizes only the first two characters of variable names, this also means that any word that starts with LI, NE, PR, or LO also is prohibited. A complete list of Applesoft Reserved Words is given in the *Applesoft Programming Reference Manual* by Apple Computer and most other programming manuals. To help keep things simple, a table of legal variable names (those you can use) is included in the appendix of this book.

Variables which contain both alphabetic and numeric information (alphanumeric) are also string variables. For example, addresses could be stored in string variables called ADDRESS$ or AD$. If the address 2130 67th Street is stored in a program it is a string variable.

Numbers are considered by the Apple to be either "real numbers," those having decimal values, or "integer numbers" which do not have decimals. Five is an integer number; 5.245677 is a real number. Integer number variables are identified by a percent sign (%) at the end. Real number variables have no special sign to identify them. N could be used to represent a real number. N% could represent an integer number. Number variables also can be named almost anything. A program that keeps track of your age might call that variable AGE%. If you wanted to be more precise, the variable name AGE could be used to store your age as 35.567432. The sample program which follows illustrates these types of variables. Enter it into your Apple and **RUN** it. Do not press RETURN at the end of the first line in statement 60 as you normally would on a typewriter. When a line is filled (39 characters), the Apple will automatically return the cursor to the left margin. Press RETURN only when you have finished typing the entire statement.

```
10 NAME$ = "BOB PRICE"
20 ADDRESS$ = "1111 ANY STREET"
30 AGE% = 36
40 HEIGHT = 5.09
50 HOME:PRINT:PRINT
60 PRINT   NAME$:PRINT   ADDRESS$:PRINT   AGE%:
   PRINT HEIGHT
```

When the program is **RUN**, it should look like this:

BOB PRICE
1111 ANY STREET
35
5.09

In lines 10 through 40, the program assigns values to variables. Line 50 clears the screen and brings the cursor down two lines from the top. Line 60 prints out the values stored in the variables. More about variables later.

The PRINT Command

PRINT is one of the most important and most often used commands. We have used it several times already. It can be used to cause whatever is within quotation marks, or the value of a variable, to be displayed on the screen when a program is **RUN**. **PRINT** can be used either in the immediate mode or as part of a program. For practice, type the following program on your Apple and **RUN** it. If you make a typing mistake, use the editing procedures previously described. Type **NEW** before you begin to tell your Apple that you're starting a new program.

```
10   PRINT "THIS IS A SAMPLE PROGRAM WHICH
     DEMONSTRATES THE PRINT COMMAND."
20   PRINT
30   PRINT "A + B"
40   PRINT
50   PRINT 2 + 2
60   PRINT
70   PRINT A + B
80   PRINT
90   PRINT 100
100  END
```

Let's take a look at how the program works. Line 10 simply causes the sentence typed inside the quotation marks to appear on the screen. Notice how the word DEMONSTRATES is divided. The Apple normally prints 39 characters per line. Because the A in DEMONSTRATES is the 39th character, the Apple does an automatic line feed at this point and continues on the next line. We'll show you how to correct this problem shortly. Lines 20, 40, 60, and 80 use the **PRINT** statement alone to cause a blank line to appear on the screen. Line 30 prints the letters A + B exactly as we have them inside the quotation marks. Line 40 causes two things to happen.

First, 2 and 2 are added together. Second, the result (4) is displayed on the screen. Can you tell why? Because A + B are not enclosed in quotation marks, the Apple assumes that A and B are variables. Given that we have assigned no value to these, the Apple automatically assigns them a value of 0. It then adds 0 + 0 and prints the result — 0.

Line 90 causes the number 100 to appear on the screen. The Apple will let you print any number. It is not necessary to enclose numbers in quotes. Line 100 is an **END** statement and tells the computer that this is the end of the program. The program would work just fine without the **END** statement, but it is considered good programming technique to include it, so it is a good idea to get in the habit of using it now.

Error Messages and Debugging

From time to time, you will enter things into your Apple that it doesn't like. Its way of telling you how it feels about this is called an "error message." If you enter **PRINY** "HELLO" instead of **PRINT** "HELLO," you will receive a message that looks like this: SYNTAX ERROR IN 100. This roughly translates to "Watch your typing!" Another of your computer's favorite things to say is ILLEGAL QUANTITY ERROR IN 100. The computer prefers to respond in obtuse ways, such as this. When you enter errors in your program, the Apple will seem to accept them, but when the program is **RUN**, the error messages will appear and the program will "bomb" or simply halt its execution at the point of the error. A big part of programming is "debugging" — that is, proceeding through the program, finding all the mistakes, and correcting them. Unless you are a much better typist than we are, never expect any program to **RUN** all the way through on the first try. When errors are revealed, **LIST** the offending line and check it carefully. If you can't find the problem, check the list of error messages given in the *Apple Programming Reference Manual* for clues to the nature of the problem.

More On the PRINT Statement

Because the arbitrary division of words at the end of a line is bothersome to most humans, we can correct this and make the print appear neater by counting the characters and putting no more than 39 in one **PRINT** statement.

Using the editing procedures previously described, line 10 in our practice program could be changed and a new line, 15, added to divide the sentence properly. With the old practice program still in your Apple's memory, enter the following two new lines:

```
10 PRINT "THIS IS A SAMPLE PROGRAM WHICH"
15 PRINT "DEMONSTRATES THE PRINT COMMAND."
```

LIST your program and you will see that the old line 10 has been deleted and the new one entered in its place and that the new line 15 has been placed in its proper sequence between lines 10 and 20. **RUN** the program and the sentence will appear properly divided on the screen.

VTAB and HTAB

The **VTAB** and **HTAB** commands work something like tabs on a typewriter to allow you to position print wherever you wish on the video screen. **VTAB** stands for vertical tab, and allows you to move the cursor to a designated vertical line. The **PRINT** statement following a **VTAB** will begin at that location. Because there is room for 24 vertical lines on your video screen, we can combine the **VTAB** command with numbers between 0 and 23. (Remember, computers like to use 0 for the first number.) Clear your Apple and enter the short program below to demonstrate **VTAB**.

```
10 TEXT:HOME
20 VTAB 12
30 PRINT "HELLO"
```

Because there is room for 24 vertical lines of print on your Apple's video screen, **VTAB** 12 is the approximate center. If we omitted the **VTAB** command, the word HELLO would appear in the upper left of the screen (line 0) when the program is **RUN**.

To center HELLO horizontally, we can use **HTAB**. **HTAB** works much like **VTAB**. Because there is room for 39 characters on each line, we can center words in the same manner as you would on a typewritten page: First, count the number of letters in the word or line you wish to center. HELLO has five letters. Second, subtract that number (5 in this case) from $39.39 - 5 = 34$. Third, divide 34 by 2 ($34/2 = 17$). 17 is the line where we need to start printing in order to center HELLO. Add the line: 25 **HTAB** 17 to your sample program and **RUN** it to demonstrate. The word HELLO should now appear centered on the video screen.

The Semicolon (;)

The Apple normally does an automatic line feed after it finishes any printing. If you have just **RUN** the sample HELLO program, the cursor should now be located on the line below the word HELLO. Sometimes we would rather not have a line feed so that we can continue printing on the same line with the next **PRINT** statement. To demonstrate, add the

semicolon (;) to the end of line 30 of our sample program, and add the
new line, 40, so that it looks like this:

```
10  TEXT:HOME
20  VTAB 12
25  HTAB 17
30  PRINT "HELLO";
40  PRINT " BOB."
```

Note the blank space before the B in BOB. The program **RUN** should
look like this:

    HELLO BOB.

Experiment with the **PRINT**, semicolon (;), **VTAB**, and **HTAB** commands until you feel comfortable with them.

The INPUT Command

Another useful and important command is **INPUT**. When an **INPUT**
command is encountered in a program, it causes the Apple to display a
question mark (?) and then pause to wait for information to be entered
from the keyboard. To enter information when the program is **RUN**, you
will type your response and press **RETURN**. The information entered can
then be used by the program. The **INPUT** command (e.g., **INPUT** A)
simply causes the program to halt and a question mark to be displayed. A
better method is to combine the **INPUT** command with a prompt or a
printed message to the user. The additions to the practice program that
follows illustrate use of the **INPUT** command. Type **NEW** and enter the
practice program below to demonstrate **INPUT**, **PRINT**, and the semicolon
(;):

```
 0  TEXT:HOME
10  PRINT "THIS IS A SAMPLE PROGRAM WHICH"
15  PRINT "DEMONSTRATES PRINT AND INPUT
      COMMANDS."
20  PRINT
25  PRINT "WHAT IS YOUR NAME?";NAME$
27  PRINT
30  PRINT "HELLO, ";NAME$;"."
40  PRINT
45  PRINT "2+2=";
50  PRINT 2 + 2
60  PRINT
65  INPUT "ENTER A VALUE FOR A:";A
```

```
67   INPUT "ENTER A VALUE FOR B:";B
68   PRINT
69   PRINT "A + B = ";
70   PRINT A + B
80   PRINT
90   PRINT "GOODBYE, ";NAME$;"."
95   PRINT
100  END
```

You will notice when you **LIST** programs, the Apple formats them to have a pleasing appearance. For example, the second line of any statement will be indented — such as line 15. Statements also will be indented two spaces from the line number to make them easier to read. This display format does not affect the operation of the program.

Before you **RUN** the program, study it and see if you can tell what each line does. Pretend that you are the computer. With a pencil and paper in hand, "execute" the program, line by line. When you are ready, **RUN** the program and see how accurate you were. If you got everything right, you have a good understanding of how the computer operates when it works in BASIC. When you run the program your screen will look like this:

THIS IS A SAMPLE PROGRAM WHICH
DEMONSTRATES PRINT AND INPUT COMMANDS.

WHAT IS YOUR NAME? BOB

HELLO, BOB.

2 + 2 = 4

ENTER A VALUE FOR A: 10
ENTER A VALUE FOR B: 20

A + B = 30

GOODBYE, BOB.

Here's how it works. Lines 10 and 15 **PRINT** our introductory sentence on the screen, dividing it nicely for a pleasing appearance. Line 25 first prints the prompt "WHAT IS YOUR NAME?" and then waits for your answer. When you type your name and press **RETURN**, your name is entered and stored in the variable labeled NAME$. In line 30, the Apple **PRINT**s your name with HELLO (e.g., HELLO, BOB.) The semicolons defeat the automatic line feeds which the Apple normally does after finishing a **PRINT** statement, so that HELLO + BOB + (.) are neatly combined together on one line. Line 45 prints $2 + 2 =$. Again, the semicolon tells the Apple to stay on the same line after this is printed. Line 50 will present the results of adding $2 + 2$ (4) beside the displayed $2 + 2$. Line 65 is another **INPUT** statement. However, this time the information requested is a number. You may enter any number. In our example we used 10. This is stored by the computer as variable A. Line 67 follows the same procedure for entering variable B. In the example, 20 was entered. Line 69 prints the message: $A + B =$. Line 70 adds the two numbers which were entered as A and B and prints the results (30 in our example). Line 90 combines your name and "GOODBYE." Line 100 ends the program.

Calculating Interest on Savings

Using the commands that we have learned thus far, plus a few others, we can use the Apple to do some neat mathemathical calculations. The next sample program will calculate interest on your savings account. **SAVE** the previous program if you wish, then type **NEW** to clear the computer's memory and enter the following program:

```
5    REM GROWTH OF SAVINGS PGM
7    TEXT : HOME : CLEAR
8    VTAB 3
10   PRINT "THIS PROGRAM COMPUTES THE TOTAL
     AMOUNT"
20   PRINT "OF MONEY YOU WILL ACCUMULATE IF YOU"
30   PRINT "INVEST A SPECIFIED AMOUNT EACH YEAR."
40   PRINT
50   INPUT "HOW MUCH WILL YOU INVEST YEARLY? ";D
60   INPUT "FOR HOW MANY YEARS WILL YOU INVEST? ";Y
70   INPUT "WHAT RATE OF INTEREST WILL YOU EARN?
     ";R
80   R = R / 100
90   HOME : VTAB 3
100  PRINT "YEAR TOTAL INVESTMENT    TTL
     ACCUMULATED"
110  PRINT
120  B = 1 + R
130  PRINT 1,D;"        ";D
140  FOR L = 1 TO Y
150  B = B * (1 + R)
160  S = (D * (B - 1) ) / R
170  IF L < Y THEN PRINT L + 1, (L + 1) * D;"      ";S
```

```
180 NEXT L
190 END
```

RUN

A **RUN** of the program looks like this:

THIS PROGRAM COMPUTES THE TOTAL AMOUNT
OF MONEY YOU WILL ACCUMULATE IF YOU
INVEST A SPECIFIED AMOUNT EACH YEAR.

HOW MUCH WILL YOU INVEST YEARLY? 600

FOR HOW MANY YEARS WILL YOU INVEST? 10

WHAT RATE OF INTEREST WILL YOU RECEIVE? 9

YEAR	TOTAL INVESTMENT	TTL ACCUMULATED
1	600	600
2	1200	1254
3	1800	1966.86
4	2400	2743.8775
5	3000	3590.82637
6	3600	4514.0073
7	4200	5520.2608
8	4800	6617.08428
9	5400	7812.62186
10	6000	9115.75783

   RUN the program once with exactly the same information given in the sample and check to see that your data is the same. Following the editing procedures described earlier in this chapter, correct any errors you made while entering the program.
   Let's look at how the program works. Line 5 is a **REMARK** statement, **REM** for short. **REMS** are used to label or identify programs or to leave messages for any humans who may look at them. They cause no action on the part of the Apple. The computer simply ignores them. In this case, we used a **REM** (line 5) to give the program a name. Lines 10 through 70 are **PRINT** and **INPUT** statements. Line 80 converts the interest rate in percent, in this case 9%, to a decimal value (that is, .09). Line 100 prints the column headers. The rest of the program does the math for us and prints the results on the screen.

Line 130 prints the first row figures — year 1, 600, 600. Lines 140-180 are called a "loop." This part of the program figures the year (variable Y), the total investment (L + 1)XD, and the total accumulated for each year (variable S). It's beyond our scope here to explain just how these mathematical formulas work. Let's just say that formulas exist for doing about anything that you might want your Apple to do. Many formulas are given in the *Apple Programming Reference Manual* and other programming manuals.

Because the program is called on to make repetitive, routine calculations, the computer uses this part of the program over and over. Y represents the number of years in our analysis, in the example 10. Line 140 says that we will go through the loop Y number of times. Line 180, **NEXT L**, tells the computer that this is the end of the loop and to go back to do it again until L = Y (or 10). When 10 (for 10 years) is reached, the program goes on to line 190, which ends the program. (The program assumes that simple annual interest is paid and is compounded yearly.)

To illustrate another programming concept, let's add a few more lines to the program:

```
190  INPUT "DO YOU WISH ANOTHER CALCULATION?
     ";ANSWER$
200  IF ANSWER$ = "YES" THEN RUN
210  END
```

Rather than end the program after one calculation, the program will now give the user a chance to repeat the process. The key to this is line 200. This is called an **IF/THEN** statement. It allows the computer to evaluate a response and act accordingly. Experiment with the program. **RUN** it several times with different figures. Can you think of ways to improve it? Save the program when you are through.

READ/DATA

So far, we have seen only one way to enter data into a computer program — the **INPUT** command. Another means of data entry is illustrated by the following program, which converts fahrenheit temperatures to centigrade. Enter the program into your computer and check carefully for errors.

```
1   REM FAHRENHEIT/CENTIGRADE PGM
10  TEXT : CLEAR : HOME
20  PRINT : PRINT "THIS PROGRAM CONVERTS
    FAHRENHEIT": PRINT "TEMPERATURES
    TO CENTIGRADE."
```

```
22 PRINT
25 PRINT "PRESS ANY KEY TO CONTINUE: ": GET X$
27 PRINT "FAHRENHEIT", "CENTIGRADE"
30 READ F
35 IF F = 1000 THEN END
40 C = (F − 32) * (5 / 9)
50 PRINT "F = ";F,"C = ";C
60 GOTO 30
70 DATA 5,10,15,20,25,30,32,35,40,45,50,55,60
80 DATA 65,70,75,80,85,90,95,100,1000
90 END
```

A **RUN** of the program will look like this:

F = 5	C = − 15
F = 10	C = − 12.2222222
F = 15	C = − 9.44444445
F = 20	C = − 6.66666667
F = 25	C = − 3.88888889
F = 30	C = − 1.11111111
F = 32	C = 0
F = 35	C = 1.66666677
F = 40	C = 4.44444445
F = 45	C = 7.22222223
F = 50	C = 10
F = 55	C = 12.7777778
F = 60	C = 15.5555556
F = 65	C = 18.3333333
F = 70	C = 21.1111111
F = 80	C = 26.6666667
F = 85	C = 29.4444444
F = 90	C = 32.2222222
F = 95	C = 35
F = 100	C = 37.7777778

When the program comes to the **READ** statement in line 30, it looks for the first item from the first **DATA** statement. The computer takes the values from the **DATA** statement and assigns them sequentially to the variable F (for Fahrenheit). When all the data from the first **DATA** statement has been used, the program automatically looks for the second data statement. The number 1000 at the end of line 80 is used as a flag to signal that there is no more data. Line 35 is an **IF/THEN** statement which continually looks for 1000. When found, the program ends. Data statements can be placed anywhere in the program, but are usually located at the end of the program.

GOTO and GOSUB

One of the greatest things about computers is their ability to go around in circles. The commands **GOTO** and **GOSUB** are used to break the normal sequence of program instructions. We have seen it used several times already. Line 60 in the temperature conversion program is a **GOTO** statement. It is used to keep the program looping back to line 30.

GOSUB is much like a **GOTO** except for one difference — the computer remembers where it departed from the normal sequence. When it encounters a **RETURN**, it goes gack to the next line after the **GOSUB**. **GOSUBS** are used when one part of the program, called a subroutine, is used at more than one place in the program.

The following program illustrates the use of **GOSUB, GOTO, IF/THEN**, and **FOR/NEXT** loops. Clear your computer, type the program, list it and check for errors.

```
10   REM   MATH DRILL
20   TEXT : CLEAR : HOME
30   PRINT : PRINT
40   PRINT "ADDITION AND MULTIPLICATION DRILL"
50   PRINT
60   PRINT "ENTER YOUR CHOICE:": PRINT
70   PRINT"        1 = ADDITION"
80   PRINT"        2 = MULTIPLICATION"
90   PRINT"        3 = QUIT"
100  PRINT
110  INPUT "ENTER YOUR CHOICE: ";N
120  IF N = 1 THEN GOTO 200
130  IF N = 2 THEN GOTO 300
140  IF N = 3 THEN GOTO 400
150  IF N > 3 THEN GOTO 10
160  REM RANDOM NUMBER SELECTION
170  A = INT ( RND (1) * 10)
180  B = INT ( RND (1) * 10)
190  RETURN
200  REM ADDITION SUBROUTINE
202  HOME
205  PRINT "ADDITIONAL DRILL"
210  FOR I = 1 TO 10
```

```
220 GOSUB 160
230 PRINT : PRINT : PRINT A;" + ";B;" = ";
250 INPUT X
260 IF X = (A + B) THEN PRINT "THAT IS CORRECT."
270 IF X < > (A + B) THEN PRINT "THAT IS NOT RIGHT."
275 FOR PAUSE = 1 TO 1000: NEXT
280 NEXT I
290 GOTO 10
300 REM MULTIPLICATION SUBROUTINE
303 HOME
305 PRINT "MULTIPLICATION DRILL"
310 PRINT
320 FOR I = 1 TO 10
330 GOSUB 160
340 PRINT : PRINT A;"X";B;" = ";
350 INPUT X
355 PRINT
360 IF X = (A * B) THEN PRINT "THAT IS RIGHT."
370 IF X < > (A * B) THEN PRINT "SORRY,
    THAT IS NOT CORRECT."
380 PRINT "TRY THIS ONE."
385 NEXT I
390 GOTO 10
400 REM END ROUTINE
410 HOME
420 VTAB 12: PRINT "THANKS FOR PRACTICING
    YOUR MATH WITH ME."
430 END
```

Before you **RUN** the program, see if you can tell how it works and what it does. All of the commands have been covered.

For review, we'll look at how the program works. Line 10 is a **REM** statement that causes no action from the computer. It identifies the program. Line 20 does a little housekeeping for us by making sure that the computer is in the **TEXT** mode and by clearing the screen. Lines 30 to 100 print the "menu." Line 110 lets you enter 1, 2, or 3 as variable N. Lines 120-150 evaluate our choice and send us either to line 200 for addition drill, 300 for subtraction drill, or 400 to quit. If we make a mistake and enter a number greater than 3, line 150 sends us back to the start of the program.

If we choose 1, the program "branches" to line 200. Line 202 clears the screen. Line 205 prints a title on the screen. Line 210 starts a loop which will be repeated 10 times. Line 220 branches to 160, where a subroutine randomly picks two random numbers between 1 and 10. Line 230 prints the problem on the screen. The semicolon (;) defeats the line feed which otherwise would occur. Line 250 causes the Apple to pause and wait for an answer which is entered as variable X. Lines 260-270 evaluate our answer in **IF/THEN** statements. If the answer given is right, a reinforcing message is printed on the screen. If the answer given is wrong, then we are so advised. Because the answer must be either right or wrong, the appropriate response is always printed. Line 275 causes the computer to pause momentarily. The length of the pause can be controlled by changing the number 1000 after FOR PAUSE = 1 TO 1000 in line 275. Line 280 tells the computer to repeat this sequence of instructions. This is repeated until X = 10 (when 10 problems have been attempted).

Line 400 starts the end routine. Line 410 clears the screen. Line 420 prints the message "THANKS FOR PRACTICING YOUR MATH WITH ME." Line 420 ends the program.

Can you think of ways to "enhance" the program? When you are finished, save the program on your disk or tape.

This chapter has covered quick and dirty BASIC. There is much that has not been said. The purpose here was not to make you a proficient programmer, but rather to give you an idea of how computer programming works. As mentioned earlier, there are many good programming manuals for Apple users. Many books on Apple BASIC are probably available at your local bookstore. In Chapter 6, we will look at how to use BASIC to create graphics.

Chapter 6

Programming Graphics and Sound

The Apple can produce two types of graphics — low-resolution graphics and high-resolution graphics. These modes were discussed in Chapter 2. If you have forgotten what is meant by low- and high-resolution graphics, it would be a good idea to review Chapter 2 at this time. We also assume that you have read Chapter 5.

Both graphics modes produce brilliant colors, but you can see them only if you have a color video display. Drawing pictures on your video display is much like working on a piece of graph paper. In the low-resolution graphics mode, the screen has an invisible 40 × 40 grid superimposed on it. (See Figure 2.2.) Graphics are drawn by filling blocks of color on the grid. High-resolution graphics work the same way except that the grid is 280 horizontal columns by 160 vertical rows. This makes the blocks on the grid much smaller than they are in low-resolution graphics, thus much greater detail is possible. There are only a few commands for each mode. A little practice with these and soon you'll be programming in color.

LOW-RESOLUTION GRAPHICS

Here is a summary of the commands needed to program low-resolution pictures:

GR. This tells the Apple that you wish to work in the low-resolution mode. It converts the screen to an invisible 40 × 40 grid, clears it to black, and leaves space for four lines of normal text display at the bottom of the screen. Grid squares are numbered 0 to 39, not 1 to 40.

COLOR = X. This sets the color. The X represents a number betwen 0 and 15. A table of colors is given in Chapter 2. The default color is black. Once a color is selected, it remains unchanged until it is changed

FIGURE 6.1 An example of a low res graphics display.

with another **COLOR** command. The command **COLOR = 2** will cause squares plotted with commands which follow to be blue.

PLOT X,Y. Places a colored square at horizontal grid coordinate X and vertical grid coordinate Y. Both X and Y are from 0 to 39. (See the low-resolution grid graphic in Chapter 2). The command **PLOT** 0,0 will place a colored square in the upper left corner of the grid.

HLIN X1,X2 AT Y. Draws horizontal lines from the point X1 to X2 on horizontal line Y. The command **HLIN** 0,39 **AT** 20 will draw a horizontal line across the center of the screen from column 0 to column 39 at vertical row 20.

VLIN Y1,Y2 AT X. Draws a vertical line from the point Y1 to Y2 on vertical line X. The command **VLIN** 0,39 **AT** 20 will draw a vertical line across the center of the screen from row 0 to row 39 at horizontal column 20.

That's all there is to it! These few commands, combined with the programming techniques covered in Chapter 5, are all you need to draw screen graphics for your programs. Boot and clear your Apple and let's get started.

Drawing a Frame Around The Screen

Enter the following program and **RUN** it. It will produce a nice medium blue frame around your TV screen.

```
10 REM FRAME
20 GR : COLOR= 6
30 HLIN 0,39 AT 0: VLIN 0,39 AT 0
40 HLIN 0,39 AT 39: VLIN 0,39 AT 39
```

Line 10 identifies the program. Line 20 sets the low-resolution graphics mode and sets the color to six (medium blue). Line 30 draws a horizontal line across the top of the screen and then down the left side. Line 40 draws lines across the bottom and down the right side of the screen. Because the low-resolution graphic mode leaves room for four lines of text at the bottom of the screen, you may still see some of your program or whatever else you might have had on the screen before you ran the program. The usual text commands still work for these four lines only. To demonstrate, add the following lines to your program. First enter **TEXT** and **HOME** to clear the screen, then **LIST** your program. (Don't be alarmed when you see a lot of reverse image garbage on your screen when you enter the **TEXT** command. This is normal.) Add the following lines:

```
50 HOME
60 VTAB 23: HTAB 17: PRINT "FRAME"
```

When you **RUN** the program again, you will see the word FRAME displayed in the center of the space below the frame. Applesoft BASIC will not allow you to place print directly on the graphic grid (i.e., above the four lines of text at the bottom of the screen).

We can use the **PLOT**, **HLIN**, and **VLIN** commands to draw pictures. Type **TEXT** and **HOME** again. Without clearing the program, add the following lines to your program to demonstrate.

```
65   COLOR= 15
70   HLIN 15,25 AT 10: HLIN 15,25 AT 25
80   VLIN 10,25 AT 15: VLIN 10,25 AT 25
85   COLOR= 12
90   PLOT 17,13: PLOT 23,13: PLOT 20,17
95   COLOR= 1
100  HLIN 17,23 AT 22
```

When the program is **RUN**, the results should be a little face. Can you enhance the program? Can you change the color of the eyes? Can you add a stick figure body?

Bar Graph

So far we've made some colored lines, a frame, and a face. These are amusing but have little value. The program which follows is more practical.

It asks the user to enter numbers and then plots them on a bar graph. The numbers could represent anything from the national debt to a set of scores on a spelling test. All of the commands used have been discussed previously. Enter the program exactly as it is listed and check carefully for errors before you read further.

```
10   REM BAR GRAPH PROGRAM
20   REM BY ROBERT V. PRICE
30   REM
40   TEXT : HOME
50   VTAB 3: HTAB 10: PRINT "BAR GRAPH PROGRAM"
60   VTAB 5: INPUT "NAME OF BAR GRAPH = = >";NAME$
70   PRINT : INPUT "HOW MANY PLOTS DO YOU WISH (1-7)
     = = >";P%
80   IF P% >7 THEN PRINT CHR$ (7): GOTO 70
90   PRINT : PRINT "ENTER VALUES TO BE PLOTTED
     (MAXIMUM 39):"
100  FOR X = 1 TO P%
110  PRINT
120  PRINT "ENTER VALUE ";X;" TO BE PLOTTED  = = >";:
     INPUT V(X)
130  IF V(X) >39 THEN PRINT CHR$ (7): GOTO 110
140  NEXT X
150  GR : COLOR = 10
160  VLIN 0,39 AT 0: HLIN 0,39 AT 39
170  FOR X = 0 TO 39 STEP 4: PLOT 1,X: NEXT X
180  COLOR = 15
190  FOR I = 1 TO P%
200  VLIN 39,(39 - V(I) ) AT (I * 5)
210  NEXT I
220  HOME : HTAB 10: PRINT NAME$
```

When the program is **RUN**, a title appears on the screen and the user is asked to enter a name for the graph. For practice, enter: LOAN BALANCE when the program asks you for the name. Next, the user is asked for the number of plots desired. Seven is the maximum number of plots allowed, so enter 7. When asked for the value for each plot, enter the numbers 39, 35, 30, 22, 15, 10, and 5 one at a time for each of the seven plots. When you are finished entering the numbers, a brightly colored bar graph will appear on the screen showing the plots of the numbers you have entered. This graph could represent the declining balance of a loan. Can you think of other figures to plot? Can you estimate the growth of your savings account and plot its growth? Run the program again and experiment.

Here's how the program works: Lines 10 through 140 ask the user to enter information. Lines 80 and 130 are "error traps." They cause the question to be repeated if the numbers entered by the user are too large. Lines 150 through 170 draw the outline of the graph on the screen. Lines 190 through 210 are a loop which draws the vertical lines for our bars. Line 220 prints the title, which was entered earlier, below the graph. Can you figure out ways to enhance the program? Can you change the colors? Could you change the program to allow more than 7 plots? Can you tell how many plots would be the maximum possible? Can you use the text space at the bottom of the graph to label it more clearly? Save your program first and then experiment and see what you can do.

ANIMATION

Animation, in low- or high-resolution graphics, can be fun and useful for games and special effects. However, we will only touch on an elementary example to provide you with the concept of how animation works. Enter the program below and **RUN** it. Then read on.

```
10   REM ANIMATED BLOCK
20   REM BY ROBERT V. PRICE
30   REM
40   TEXT : HOME : GR
50   VTAB 23: HTAB 12: PRINT "ANIMATED BLOCK"
60   HTAB 8: PRINT "PRESS CONTROL/C TO STOP"
70   FOR X = 1 TO 38
80   PLOT X,X
90   COLOR = 15: PLOT X + 1,X + 1: COLOR = 0
100  NEXT X
110  COLOR = 0: PLOT 39,39
120  FOR X = 39 to 1 STEP − 1
130  PLOT X,39
140  COLOR = 15: PLOT X − 1,38: COLOR = 0
150  NEXT X
160  COLOR = 0: PLOT 0,38
170  FOR X = 1 to 39
180  PLOT X,39 − X
190  COLOR = 0: PLOT X,39 − X: COLOR = 15
200  NEXT X
210  COLOR = 0: PLOT 39,0
220  FOR X = 39 TO 1 STEP − 1: PLOT X,0
230  GOTO 70
```

When the program is **RUN**, you should see what appears to be a moving colored block on the screen. What appears to be movement is really a matter of plotting a colored square on the low resolution grid, erasing it by coloring it black (color 0), and redrawing it on the next position on the grid. The process is continually repeated in rapid succession which gives us an illusion of motion. Here's how it works. Lines 70 through 100 "move" the block from the top left of the screen (grid coordinates 0,0) to the bottom right (grid coordinates 39,39). Line 110 "erases" the last block in the lower right corner. Lines 110 through 150 "move" the block from the lower right to the lower left corner by subtracting 1 from grid position X each time the plot is done. Lines 160 through 220 "move" the block diagonally across the screen to the upper right corner. Line 230 starts the process over again.

By experimenting, you can create different shapes by plotting them on the grid, erasing them by coloring them black, and then redrawing them at the adjacent position. Loops allow the program to repeat the process rapidly. With some time and imagination, you can make shapes which move, float, or even explode!

HIGH-RESOLUTION GRAPHICS

High-resolution graphics work very much like low-resolution. The basic commands are reviewed here.

HGR. Sets the high-resolution graphics mode (280×160 grid) and clears the grid to black. Space for four lines of text is provided at the bottom of the screen.

HGR2. Same as **HGR** except that the entire screen becomes a high-resolution grid with no space for text at the bottom of the screen. The **HGR2** grid is 280×192.

HCOLOR = X. Sets the color (0 to 7) for next plotting. The command **HCOLOR = 2** sets the color to violet. High-resolution colors are as follows: 0 = black, 1 = green, 2 = violet, 3 = white, 4 = black, 5 = orange, 6 = blue, 7 = white.

HPLOT X,Y. Places a colored dot at horizontal coordinate X and vertical coordinate Y. X is from 0 to 279. Y is from 0 to 159 in **HGR** and from 0 to 191 in **HGR2**. The command **HPLOT** 0,0 places a colored dot in the upper left corner.

HPLOT X1,Y1 TO X2,Y2. Draws a line from the point at X1,Y1 to the point at X2,Y2. This command may be extended to additional points without specifying the first coordinate. The command **HPLOT** 0,0 **TO** 279,159 draws a diagonal line from the upper left corner to the lower right corner of the screen. The subsequent command **HPLOT TO** 0,159 draws a line along the bottom of the screen from the lower right corner to the lower left corner. Several **HPLOT** commands may be chained with the word **TO** as **HPLOT** 0,0 **TO** 279,0 **TO** 279,159 **TO** 0,159 **TO** 0,0.

High-resolution graphics are truly wonderful, but you do have to make some sacrifices with them. There are fewer colors in high-resolution than in low-resolution, and they will vary according to your monitor or TV. Regular TVs may produce the correct colors only if the grid coordinates are all even numbers. This is due to the way home TVs work. To try out high-resolution graphics, enter the following little program and **RUN** it.

```
10 REM HI RES DEMO PGM
20 HGR : HCOLOR= 3
30 REM DRAWS BORDER
40 HPLOT 0,0 TO 279,0 TO 279,159 TO 0,159 TO 0,0
50 REM DRAWS X
60 HCOLOR= 5
70 HPLOT 0,0 TO 279,159: HPLOT 279,0 TO 0,159
80 END
```

Starburst

The next program uses the Apple's random number generator to make the computer create a picture. The colors, placement, and length of the lines will vary each time the program is **RUN**. The program creates original artwork designed by the computer. Save the former program if you wish, clear the computer and then enter and **RUN** the next program.

```
100 REM - - - -STARBURST- - - - - -
110 REM BY ROBERT PRICE
120 REM
130 TEXT : HOME
140 HGR :N = 0:X = 100:Y = 100
150 RC = INT (7 * RND (1) ) + 1
160 X2 = INT (279 * RND (1) )
170 Y2 = INT (158 * RND (1) )
180 HCOLOR= RC
190 HPLOT X,Y TO X2,Y2
200 N = N + 1: IF N = 150 THEN 220
210 GOTO 150
220 J = J + 1
230 HOME : VTAB 22: HTAB 15: PRINT "STARBURST "
    ;J: PRINT
```

```
240  PRINT "PRESS SPACE BAR TO REPEAT OR # TO STOP:"
     ;: GET X$
250  IF X$ = "#" THEN 270
260  GOTO 100
270  TEXT : HOME : END
```

The program draws a sort of starburst pattern over and over with a short pause between each drawing. Line 190 does the drawing using coordinates and colors picked in lines 140 to 180. The program loops through this procedure 100 times. Line 200 increases N by 1, the loop counter variable. When N reaches 100, it causes a jump to line 230, where the title is printed. The program pauses a moment before it starts over again. The program is an endless loop. You can stop it with a **CONTROL/C**.

Shapes

The next program will allow us to draw several predefined shapes using subroutines. Subroutines included will draw a box, a rectangle, and a triangle. You can customize and enhance the program by figuring out the grid coordinates for other shapes and adding them to the program.

```
1    REM SHAPE DRAWING PROGRAM
2    REM BY ROBERT V. PRICE
3    REM
10   TEXT : HOME : CLEAR
20   ONNERR GOTO 10
30   HOME : HGR : HCOLOR= 2: VTAB 21
40   PRINT "WHICH FIGURE WOULD YOU LIKE:"
50   PRINT "0 = BOX, 1 = TRIANGLE, 2 = RECTANGLE"
60   INPUT "ENTER YOUR CHOICE: ";N
80   IF N = 0 THEN 100
90   IF N = 1 THEN 200
95   IF N = 2 THEN 300
98   IF N > 2 THEN 30
100  REM BOX
110  HPLOT 0,0 TO 0,150 TO 150,150 TO 150,0 TO 0,0
120  HOME : VTAB 22: PRINT : HTAB 9: PRINT "BOX"
130  GOTO 400
200  REM TRIANGLE
210  HPLOT 140,0 TO 255,140 TO 0,140 TO 140,0
220  HOME : VTAB 22: HTAB 15: PRINT "TRIANGLE"
230  GOTO 400
300  REM RECTANGLE
```

```
310 HPLOT 20,0 TO 255,0 TO 255,140 TO 20,140 TO 20,0
320 HOME : VTAB 22: HTAB 14: PRINT "RECTANGLE"
400 END
```

Apple graphics can be very exciting. Some neat programs to help you produce good graphics are reviewed in Chapter 7.

NOISY APPLES

The Apple can produce sound in two basic ways. The "bell" is the beep you hear when you first turn on your Apple. You can add this sound to your program with the command: **PRINT CHR$ (7)**. Clear your Apple's memory and then enter and **RUN** the following program to illustrate the "bell."

```
10 REM BELL DEMONSTRATION
20 FOR X = 1 TO 10
30 PRINT CHR$(7)
40 NEXT X
50 END
```

Running this program is a good way to draw a crowd. Line 30 makes the beep. The loop between lines 20 and 40 repeats the beep 10 times. You can add the beep to many of your programs by adding this command wherever you wish. If you want more than one beep, just enclose it in a loop as we did here. Adding the line: 55 **PRINT CHR$(7)** to the shape drawing program will produce a beep just before the **INPUT** statement to alert the user to the fact that a response is expected. Other programs put beeps with error messages.

Clicks, tics, tocs, and buzzes can be generated by the magic command: **PEEK − 16336.** (**PEEK** commands call upon functions which have been built into the Apple — such as the ability to produce clicks through the speaker. See the *Applesoft Programming Reference Manual* for more information on **PEEK**s. There is no easy explanation for the number. It relates to the electronics of the computer. You'll just have to look it up when you need it. The following command will produce a tiny little click. Try it and see, but listen carefully.

```
PRINT PEEK − 16336
```

Enter the following program, and you'll have a rapid sequence of clicks that you'll have no trouble hearing. A sequence of numbers also will appear on the screen as the program is **RUN.**

```
10  S = - 16336
20  FOR CLICK = 1 TO 100
30  PRINT PEEK (S)
40  NEXT CLICK
```

PEEK **−16336** is a bother to type. One way to avoid typing it all the time is to define it in your program as a variable — like this: **S = −16336**. Now we can just type the S instead of the number.

To produce a nicer sound, change line 30 to the following:

```
30  NOISE = PEEK(S) − PEEK(S) + PEEK(S) − PEEK(S)
    + PEEK(S) − PEEK(S)
```

Different numbers of **PEEK**s in the statement will produce different sounds. In general, the fewer the number of **PEEK**s, the buzzier is the tone that is produced. Larger numbers of **PEEK**s produce higher pitches. Try **RUN**ning some variations and experiment.

Here's a sample program that demonstrates the noisemaking capabilities of the Apple:

```
10  REM NOISEMAKER
20  REM BY ROBERT PRICE
40  TEXT : CLEAR : HOME
50  S = − 16336
60  VTAB 3: PRINT "NOISEMAKER"
70  PRINT : PRINT "MENU"
80  PRINT : PRINT "0 = BEEPER"
90  PRINT : PRINT "1 = SMALL CLICK"
100 PRINT : PRINT "2 = BUZZ"
110 PRINT : PRINT "3 = HI PITCH TONE"
120 PRINT : PRINT "4 = QUIT"
130 PRINT : INPUT "ENTER YOUR CHOICE: ";N
140 IF N = 0 THEN 200
141 IF N = 1 THEN 300
142 IF N = 2 THEN 400
143 IF N = 3 THEN 500
144 IF N = 4 THEN 600
145 IF N > 4 THEN 10
200 REM BELL
210 FOR X = 1 TO 10: PRINT CHR$ (7): NEXT
220 GOTO 10
300 REM CLICK
```

```
310 PRINT PEEK (S)
315 PRINT PEEK (S)
320 GOTO 10
400 REM BUZZ
420 FOR X = 1 TO 100
426 P = PEEK (S) − PEEK (S) + PEEK (S) − PEEK (S)
430 NEXT X
432 FOR X = 1 TO 100
434 P = PEEK (S) − PEEK (S) + PEEK (S) − PEEK (S)
436 NEXT X
440 GOTO 10
500 REM HI PITCH TONE
510 FOR X = 1 TO 100
520 P = PEEK (S) − PEEK (S) + PEEK (S) − PEEK (S)
    + PEEK (S) − PEEK (S) + PEEK (S) − PEEK (S)
    + PEEK (S) − PEEK (S) + PEEK (S) − PEEK (S)
524 NEXT X
525 FOR X = 1 TO 100
526 P = PEEK (S) − PEEK (S) + PEEK (S) − PEEK (S)
    + PEEK (S) − PEEK (S) + PEEK (S) − PEEK (S)
    + PEEK (S) − PEEK (S) + PEEK (S) − PEEK (S)
530 NEXT X
550 GOTO 10
600 HOME : END
```

There are many good programs that can help the Apple user get the most from the graphics and sound capabilities of the Apple. We'll review some of these, as well as a lot of other interesting applications in the next chapter.

Chapter 7

Selecting Programs for Business and Pleasure

Software determines what your computer can do for you. Programs, or "software," as they are collectively called, are what make it all happen. One of the best reasons for buying an Apple is the vast amount of good software available for it. There are more good programs for the Apple computer than for any other computer.

The main types of software are reviewed here, and examples are given of each. Inclusion of any program does not necessarily constitute an endorsement nor does omission of any program mean that it is not considered worthwhile.

HOW TO SELECT SOFTWARE

The most effective and non-technical way to select software is to start by asking yourself, "What do I want the computer to do for me?" The answer will guide you to the software you need. You may decide that you want the Apple to help speed up your income tax preparation, or to help you do family budgeting. If you do a good deal of writing, you may want the computer to help handle your writing projects such as correspondence, reports, and club lists. If you enjoy electronic games, you will want some game programs. Once you decide what you want the computer to do for you, you will know where to start looking for software.

Having decided this, the next concern is the quality of the programs. Both the program and the instructions should be well written. Ask for demonstrations of programs at any computer store. Attend meetings of your nearest Apple Computer Club to look at programs and talk to other Apple users about them. Computer magazines, available at many computer stores and bookstores, often review new programs and are a valuable source of information about software. Reject programs if they are poorly written.

This applies not only to the program but also to its instruction manual. Much computer software is poorly done, and many manuals are hard to understand and clumsy. Software producers often make grandiose and unsupported claims for their products. Check everything out before you buy.

Compatibility is an all-important consideration in software selection. Microcomputer software must be designed to run on the Apple or you can't use it. Programs designed for TRS-80, Atari, or other computers will not work with the Apple. Each computer has its own more or less individual combination of CPU and operating system. There has been much talk about standardizing systems among the various manufacturers of microcomputers, but little progress has been made so far.

Because your Apple is a versatile device, you may custom-design a system that suits your needs. This flexibility means that all Apple systems are not alike. Variables include the amount of memory available, the type of printer (if any), number and type of disk drives, languages available, game controllers, and many other factors. All programs make certain assumptions about the computer system on which they are to be run. For instance, some Apple programs are written in the Logo language. If you do not have Logo available on your Apple, you can't run these programs. Other programs are written to work with specific types of printers. If your system doesn't have a printer attached or has a type not included in the program's options, it may not work. Some programs require two disk drives to operate. If you have only one drive, you have a problem. The system requirements should be clearly stated in the program's manual. Make sure the program fits your system before you buy.

One final word about compatibility. Much software was developed between the introduction of the original Apple II in 1974 and the IIe in 1983. The vast majority of programs developed for the Apple II and II+ will work with no problems on the IIe. One study reported by Apple Orchard magazine tested a large sample of II+ software on the IIe. They found that 78% worked just fine with no problems. Some 13% were found to have minor problems with the documentation or the keyboard, such as making reference to the **REPT** key. There is no **REPT** key on the Apple IIe. That leaves about 9% that had real problems. For example, some programs require accessories that are designed to fit in slot 0 on the II+. There is no slot 0 on the IIe, so these programs get confused and refuse to work when run on the IIe. If you are considering buying software developed prior to 1983 for a IIe, it probably will work, but check it out before you buy to be sure.

Some programs written since early 1983 are designed to take advantage of the added features available on the IIe and may not work on the II+

and II. However, because such a large number of II+s and IIs are in use, publishers would be foolish to ignore them when designing software. Therefore, most newer programs are written to work on the IIe, II+, and II. The few programs that can cause problems for the older Apples usually involve use of the expanded memory (64K is standard on the IIe while many earlier Apples have a maximum of 48K), or take advantage of the lowercase input which is present on the IIe but not the II+ or II. If you are buying programs published since early 1983 to use on an Apple II+ or II, look them over carefully before you buy just to be sure that they will work on your computer.

Once you have determined your computing needs, eliminated the poor programs and those programs that won't work with your system, there will likely still be many programs from which to choose. For instance, there are at least 30 word-processing programs for the Apple computer and hundreds of games available. Four factors should be considered in determining which program is best for you:

Factor 1:   Power

Power refers to what programs can do. Some programs do a lot. Others don't do as much but are easier to master and use, and cost less. As a general rule, the greater the power of the program, the more complex it is and therefore the more difficult to learn and use. More powerful programs also cost more. Buy programs to fit your needs. If you are looking for a new game, don't get a simple, cheap game that you will be bored with after a few minutes of play. If you go shopping for a word processor for the preparation of your club newsletter, don't get the most expensive and complex word processor available because it will cost more than you need to spend, have many features that you won't use, and be difficult to master.

Factor 2:   Replacement and Guarantee

The publisher's replacement policy could mean extra costs to you if you buy a program which later develops a flaw or becomes damaged. Some publishers furnish you with an extra backup copy of the program when you purchase it. Others will allow you to purchase backups at a reduced rate. Still others ask you to return damaged disks for replacement at no charge. Some publishers do not provide backups or have no clearly defined policy on the matter. Check out the replacement policy before you buy.

Some publishers have a satisfaction guaranteed policy: That is, they will allow you to return the program within a specified period of time if you aren't happy with it. Most publishers don't do this. Don't expect to find guarantees with inexpensive programs. But if a program has a satisfaction guarantee, you can feel assured that the publisher has confidence in the product.

Factor 3:   Ease of Use

Some programs just aren't easy to use. Poorly written instructions are a common problem. We have seen many excellent programs that come with instructions that are nearly impossible to understand. Some programs are awkward to use even when you do figure them out. Action games that use keyboard control are an example of difficult-to-use programs. Word-processing programs which require several keystrokes to perform simple tasks invite the user to make excessive errors and take more time to use.

PROGRAMS FOR BUSINESS AND PROFESSIONAL USES

There are three general categories of use for the small computer in business — word processing, financial planning, and data management. A brief review of these and some of the programs available for each use follows. The producer, minimum hardware requirements, and approximate cost are given for each program.

Word Processing

Word processing is probably the most popular business use for small computers. If you often write reports, term papers, newsletters, proposals, letters, lists, or almost any other type of written information, you need word processing. Word processing is a neat and efficient way to prepare written materials such as these. By streamlining the time-consuming drudgery of making corrections and changes, written materials can be generated much faster and easier. A word processor is a program, usually on a diskette, which turns your computer into a powerful, computerized electric typewriter. As you type, your words appear on the video screen, instead of on paper. Word processors make it possible to easily correct typing and other errors before your document is printed on paper. Paragraphs can be moved around or deleted. New sentences or words can be inserted in the middle of previously written material. Figures can be changed easily. Mistakes and changes like these no longer mean time-consuming and tedious retyping. Your letters, reports and other printed materials can be stored on disk and recalled to be edited or printed at any time. There are at least 30 word-processing programs for the Apple, ranging in price from $50 to $500 with a variety of features to satisfy almost any need. Here are some of the good ones:

Bank Street Writer. This is an extremely easy-to-use program designed for kids. However, its features make it adequate for many adults as well. The manual is short and well written, and a tutorial on use of the program is included on the disk. Simple and easy-to-follow directions are included in the program. The program is flexible enough to work with most popular printers. Some features of the program are the ability to automatically center headings, justify margins, and set variable line spacing. This is an excellent program for general home use. Kids can prepare their reports for school on it, and Mom and Pop can keep their Christmas card list on it or write their letters with it. Uncomplicated business uses such as preparing simple inventory lists, memos, and short reports also are easily done with Bank Street Writer. If you have kids and a computer or if simplicity and ease of use are the most important considerations, Bank Street Writer is a good program for you.

Broderbund Software; 48K memory, one disk drive, printer; cost $70.

Format II. This extremely powerful program includes the capability to easily generate form letters and labels. It also can sort information based on such variables as zip codes, an unusual feature for a word processor. Long reports are easily handled by Format II. It can be used with advanced printer functions such as underlining and boldface type. The manual is complete and easy to use. The program comes with a self-running demonstration program on disk. Format II can be used with one or two disk drive systems. It requires 64K of memory, lowercase capability, and 80-column display capability. (These features are standard on the IIe, but are optional on the II+ and II.)

Kensington Microware; 64K, one disk drive, 80-column display capability, lowercase capability, printer; $150.

Executive Secretary. This is a sophisticated program that provides all the usual capabilities of word processors as well as advanced features such as printing on preprinted forms, index alphabetizing, card file maintenance, file merging, and electronic mail. For such as sophisticated program, it is fairly easy to use, although the user should plan to spend a day or two practicing with the manual before serious use is attempted. Executive Secretary comes with a single-wire shift key modification which must be installed inside the Apple II+ or II to use the **SHIFT** key for capitalization. The program is good for operations like mass mailings, formal reports, manuals, and manuscripts, but it is not the best choice for simpler uses.

Sof/Sys; 48k, one disk drive, printer; $100.

Spelling Checkers

A good companion to a word-processor program is a spelling checker. If you are an excellent speller and a superior typist, you probably don't need a spelling checker, but if you sometimes misspell words or make typing mistakes, a spelling checker provides a way to proofread your documents quickly and easily. Spelling checkers check the documents you have written with a word processor and stored on disk. They compare the words in your document against a dictionary on another disk and identify any words that are not in the dictionary.

Sensible Speller IV. One good spelling checker program is Sensible Speller IV by Sensible Software. The program comes with a disk dictionary of more than 80,000 words. It is fast and easy to use. The program allows you to add new words to the dictionary. Options include the capability to print a list of misspelled words to a printer. The program can replace misspelled words with the proper spelling, or suggest correct spellings for your mistakes. Several other spelling checker programs are available for the Apple. However, none of the others we have seen can compare to Sensible Speller IV in terms of speed of operation, dictionary size, and flexibility of use.

Sensible Software; 48K, one disk drive; under $100.

Financial Planning

Computers are great for doing arithmetic — simple or complex. They are fast and accurate. Office applications include maintaining records of accounts, estimating costs of work to be performed, and general accounting. Many good programs are available to help you and your Apple compute and keep track of all the figures.

VisiCalc. More copies of VisiCalc have been sold than any other business computer program. A sophisticated electronic spreadsheet, VisiCalc can handle virtually any problem you would explore using a calculator or pencil and paper, working in rows and columns. It gives you an electronic worksheet of 64 columns by 254 rows, and is a powerful tool for financial analysis or business modeling. The popularity of VisiCalc has spawned many similar programs from other producers.

VisiCorp; 48K, one disk drive; $150.

BPI Job Cost. This program, by BPI Inc., helps contractors estimate and control job costs. Labor and material files, each containing many separate cost elements, may be set up by the user. Overhead rates and escalation rates also may be defined by the user. "What if" questions may be answered by changing any cost element or rate. Up-to-date reports may be generated by percentage of the job completed which includes materials and hours used and dollar balances. The program can save the contractor much time in calculating costs for preparation of bids and can help eliminate cost overruns.

BPI Inc.; 48K, two disk drives, printer; under $200.

BPI General Ledger Accounting. This program, also from BPI Inc., is designed to handle many aspects of business accounting. The program can be used to post and print ledgers, maintain employee earnings records, prepare balance sheets, and prepare profit and loss statements.

BPI Inc.; 48K, two disk drives, printer; under $200.

AccRec. This is a time recorder and wage summary program for use in small businesses. Employees enter a personal ID code to clock in and out. The program displays daily and weekly records, and eliminates time-consuming conversion of time cards into paychecks. Reports generated include an accurate record of attendance and gross wages for each employee. Overtime rates, paydays, and workweek structure may be set by the user.

Individualized Operand; 48K, one disk drive, printer; $80.

MicroFinesse. An unusual feature of this program is the ability to print color high-resolution graphics such as charts, histograms, and graphs for the financial projections you create. Up to 15 different types of reports, with visuals, can be printed on your printer. The program allows the user to put financial information in polished, professional-looking, and easy-to-understand form.

Osborne/McGraw-Hill; 48K, one disk drive, printer; under $100.

Data Management

Managing data with a computer is like having a computerized filing cabinet. All businesses store and retrieve information — on employees, customers, supplies, products, etc. In a conventional business, this type of information is typed or written by hand, stored in a filing cabinet in some sort of logical order, and retrieved by hand — if it can be found. A computer can make this process faster and more accurate while it also consumes less space and makes the information easier to retrieve. Several general data base management programs exist that are flexible enough to be used in a wide variety of applications. Many specialized versions of data base managers also have been written for specialized applications such as keeping medical records in a doctor's office, or managing real estate. Here are some data base management programs for the Apple.

DB Master III. DB Master III is a flexible data base management program which is perfect for keeping inventories or keeping records on clients and customers. The program user may elect to set up records in a variety of formats. A user doing inventory control might set up records on 100 different types of merchandise. The type and amount of information on each could vary. For example, price, source, and date of acquisition can be recorded. The user also may design customized reports and display screens. Files may be protected by a password. Files may be searched on any one or a combination of several fields. If you should desire a list of all your inventory purchased from one source, DB Master could oblige easily. If you desired a list of the inventory purchased on a certain date, the information could be retrieved easily. By searching on more than one field, you could locate all items purchased on a specific date, from a specific supplier, within a specific price range.

Stoneware; 48K, two disk drives; $150.

Datatree. Datatree helps you organize, search, update, sort, and print out detailed information. With it, you can format and maintain a wide variety of data, including client lists, mailing lists, bibliographies, job estimates, patient records, and inventories of business and personal items. The program comes with five demonstration programs to provide the user with hands-on practice in setting up a data base as well as a tutorial program. The program is powerful and sophisticated.

Apple Computer; 64K, two disk drives; under $200.

Inventory Manager. While the two general data base programs discussed previously can be used to keep inventories, this program is designed for this task only. The program keeps inventory statistics, vendors, reorder data, and back orders. It also can be used to generate reports and make calculations. With one disk, the program can handle up to 800 items; with two disks, it can handle up to 2,300 items.

Synergistic Software; 48K, one disk drive; $150.

Mailing List Data Base. This specialized data base program is the cat's meow of mailing list programs. Updating and additions are easy. Three separate formats of labels are possible. Up to 1,700 records may be stored on a two-disk system. Labels can be sorted on several search codes such as zip code or last name.

Synergistic Software; 48K, one disk drive; $150.

Hundreds of business programs are available for the Apple. The programs discussed here are a tiny sample. If you don't see the program you need, you'll learn about where to find more information in Chapter 8.

EDUCATIONAL PROGRAMS

The Apple is a great teaching tool. The infinite patience of the computer combined with the wide variety of educational software make computers an ideal tool for individualized instruction. There is more educational computer software available for the Apple than for any other microcomputer. Educational programs, often called courseware, are of three primary types: drill and practice, simulation and games, and tutorials.

Drill and Practice

All of us have, at one time or another, had to spend some dull, tedious hours memorizing spelling words, multiplication tables, or the like. Reciting and writing these repeatedly may be effective, but it is certainly boring. The computer can make this type of learning fun (well, almost). Through use of color graphics and sound, pacing material to the level of the user, and constant reinforcement, practicing your math can become almost bearable. Sometimes drill and practice programs are placed in a game or simulation format to make them even more interesting. Four educational drill and practice programs are reviewed here as examples.

Master Type. This program consists of 17 progressive lessons that help students master typing at their own rate. It incorporates exciting visual and sound effects that are similar to those found in video games. The program introduces the keyboard progressively through the lessons and provides typing practice gradually building up from the simple to the more complex. The learner is given a report of the number of words typed per minute and how many errors were made after each drill.

Lightning Software; 48K, one disk drive; under $40.

Supermath. This program provides drill and practice in addition, subtraction, multiplication, and division. Numbers are displayed in large colorful graphics. The learner may choose the number, type, and difficulty of problems to be solved. Users may work through the problems as fast or as slowly as they wish. Each response is reinforced by the computer with one of a variety of phrases such as "you're great." Wrong answers are responded to with phrases such as "no, try again." The learner gets two chances at each problem before the computer provides the answer. At the

end of each drill, you get a summary of the number of problems worked, and the number correct and incorrect. The program is one of four programs on a disk called "Elementary My Dear Apple."
Apple Computer, 32K, one disk drive; $30.

Spelling Tutor. Designed for third-grade through adult levels, this program uses a "flash card system" to build visual memory by providing drill and practice in spelling. Words are displayed on the screen and then disappear. The operator then types the word. The program comes with six word files for abilities from beginner to ace speller. Teachers or parents may easily add their own word files. Records are kept of the student's progress.
Sunbelt Computing; 32K, one disk drive; $20.

History and Geography Package. This program asks questions on basic American history and geography facts such as states, capitals, presidents, and countries. Score is kept and answers are reinforced appropriately by the computer. The program comes with a Revolutionary War Quiz program where two players compete when answering questions.
Micro Learningware; 32K, one disk drive; under $25.

Educational Games

Kids love to play games. (So do most adults.) Pac Man, Donkey Kong, and Raster Blaster are popular computer games, but there are also games that are educational as well as fun. Here are a few of them:

Don't Fall. This is a word guessing game from Apple Computer. Several categories of vocabulary words such as birds, states, and sports are included. The user may select the level of difficulty. The computer picks the words and the player guesses the letters. With each missed letter a figure, shown in low-resolution graphics, takes a step closer to a cliff. If all the letters of the word are guessed correctly before the figure reaches the edge of the cliff, then the player wins. If not, the player loses that round and the figure falls. Don't Fall is fun and is a good way to increase vocabulary and spelling skills. The program is included on the "Elementary My Dear Apple" disk with three other programs.
Apple Computer, 32K, one disk drive; $30.

Multiplication Bingo. This program is a basic drill and practice program combined with a bingo game. A colored bingo card is displayed on the screen. Basic multiplication problems are presented on the screen below it. For each problem answered correctly, one of the bingo squares is colored in. The player who gets all the squares colored has a bingo, and the Apple responds with a tune and some flashy graphics. This program is a noncommercial program from Computer Using Educators (CUE). The disk, titled Apple Dissemination Disk Number 3, contains several other educational programs.

CUE; 32K, one disk drive; $10.

Simulations

Simulations are programs that produce a simulation of some real process. By placing the user in the picture, so to speak, he or she becomes vicariously involved with the program. Learning can be made to seem closer to reality in this manner as well as more fun.

Adventures Around the World. This program helps children in grades 3 through 6 develop reading skills by participating in reading adventures, complete with pictures, with the Apple as guide. Questions to monitor comprehension are placed throughout the program. Four "trips" are included with the program — Let's Take an African Safari, Climbing Mount Everest, A Frozen Trip to Antarctica, and Journey Under the Sea.

Orange Cherry Media; 32K, one disk drive; under $70.

Oregon. This program takes the user on a simulated covered wagon trip across the western United States in 1847. Random bad guys, hostile Indians, and bad weather are likely to be encountered. The user makes decisions, much as the real settlers of the West did, on such things as when to stop at a fort and how much food and ammunition to buy. A combination of the decisions made by the user and random chance determine whether you successfully make it to Oregon — just as in the real days of the old West. This social studies simulation can help make history meaningful. The program is on a disk titled Elementary Volume 6 along with several other social studies simulation programs.

Minnesota Educational Computing Consortium (MECC); 32K, one disk drive; $30.

Stock Market Tycoon. You can learn the workings of the stock market while playing this game. Sound and graphics sweep you into action. Your stocks may soar or your dollars may fade away depending on the decisions you make and the wiles of the market.

Micro Program Designs; 32K, one disk drive; $30.

Tutorials

Tutorial programs lead the user through a sequence of instructions on a particular subject. Sometimes various aspects of games, simulations, or drills will be included also. Questions to determine the user's mastery of the information presented by the program usually are included. The computer acts as the user's personal teacher as he or she is guided through the information at a pace set by the learner.

How to Program in BASIC. Can you imagine a better way to learn how to program than letting your computer teach you? This program is a comprehensive tutorial on BASIC programming techniques. Instructions, samples, problems, and tests are included. A workbook and two disks are included.

Sterling Swift Publishing Company; 32K, one disk drive; $75.

Basic Electricity. This program, designed for children in grades 2 through 8, introduces the student to the fundamental aspects of electricity. It also stimulates logical thinking. The user must solve a switch problem based on the information presented.

Ideatech Company; 48K, one disk drive; under $20.

Library Skills. This program, for children in grades 3 and up, describes what is in the library and how to find it. Use of the card catalog, common reference materials, and the Dewey decimal system of classification are included. Several tutorial lessons, each followed by a number of exercises to reinforce the material presented, are featured.

Micro Power and Light Company; 32K, one disk drive; $25.

Other Educational Programs

Logo. Logo is a computer language for children. It is easy to learn and a fun way to introduce young children to the computer and programming. If you have a computer and young children, you need Logo. Through Logo, children learn how to control the computer. They also can learn problem solving, geometry, and graphic design. Logo uses a "turtle" — a graphic semblance of a real turtle which the user may direct around the high-resolution screen. Children usually start out drawing squares and other geometric shapes and progress to more complex designs. Shapes may be saved on disk, and later rearranged and combined.

There are several versions of Logo available. Apple Logo is a versatile and flexible version of the language from Apple Computer. Krell Logo, by Krell Software Company, is less powerful but simpler to master than Apple Logo. These programs will cost from $70 to $200.

FIGURE 7.1 Logo.

Apple Grade Book. Computers are great tools to help teachers keep records and average grades. This program is a grade-recording system for teachers. Student names and grades can be entered and saved on disk. Class rosters are automatically alphabetized and grades averaged. Class records can be updated easily. Individual reports and class records can be printed on your printer.

J & S Software; 48K, one disk drive, printer; $30.

Hundreds of other educational programs have been written for the Apple and more are being introduced every day. Not all will fall neatly into the categories listed here, but perhaps this sampling will give you a good idea of what the Apple can do as a teacher. Explore your local Apple computer store or write to the software vendors listed at the end of this chapter for information on other educational programs.

Teacher's Helper. This is a collection of short programs that can help any teacher. Programs include: a test maker that produces multiple choice tests from questions entered by the teacher; a class list alphabetizer; a grade averaging program; and several other neat little programs.

Sunbelt Computing; 32K, one disk drive, printer; $30.

PROGRAMS FOR HOME USE

The programs in this section are intended to help improve your quality
of life. The Apple can help you manage your personal finances. It can
store and retrieve personal information, entertain adults and kids alike,
and it can expand your learning horizons.

Many of the programs listed under the business and professional uses
section of this chapter could be used at home as well. You could, for
example, write your Aunt Sally using a word processor or keep your
Christmas card list on a data base program. However, the programs listed
in this section are designed specifically for personal use.

Micro Cookbook and Micro Barmate. Micro Cookbook includes recipes,
nutrition guides, a calorie counter, and other food related information, and
offers the user the convenience of easily entering one's own recipes. Recipes
can be located by name, category, or available ingredients. In other words,
you can tell the computer what ingredients are on hand or what type of
meal you want, and it will select the recipes you can make.

A companion program is Micro Barmate, which allows the user to select
a drink based on the ingredients on hand or by category — for example,
all mixed drinks with vodka. It also features a holiday beverage guide and
a tutorial on how to make your own liqueurs.

Virtual Combinatics; 32K, one disk drive; $30 each program.

The Genealogist's Right Hand. This is a program that maintains a record
of family relationships among large numbers of people. It stores information
about each person and produces reports such as family trees and pedigree
charts. You may select and sort people by any information you have in
your system and print out customized lists.

User Friendly Systems; 48K, one disk drive; under $100.

Household Inventory. You can keep accurate records of your household
items with this program. The program can keep track of serial numbers,
replacement costs and more. The inventory can be updated easily and
printed. These records can be extremely helpful in case of the need to file
an insurance claim or prepare a loan application.

SFA Enterprises; 32K, one disk drive, printer; $30.

The Home Accountant. This program maintains up to 100 budget
categories, and keeps track of up to five checkbooks. A personal balance
sheet and a net worth statement can be generated and printed. Credit cards
and cash transactions as well as other liabilities and expenses can be
handled. The program maintains a transaction history and provides the

option to print trend analysis and bar and line graphs of financial data.
Continental Software, 48K, one disk drive; $75.

Investment Decisions. This program will produce loan amortization schedules, annuity schedules, projected saving schedules, net value records, and other analyses based on your input. If you'd like to know how much that car loan is really costing or how much money you'll accumulate at a specified rate of interest with regular deposits, this program is for you. The program is included in the book, *Programming the Apple* by John Campbell, or it may be purchased separately on disk.
Mesa Research; 48K, one disk drive; about $50.

32 BASIC Programs for the Apple Computer. This set of 32 programs includes programs to balance your checkbook, calculate loan payments, analyze your gas mileage, and chart your biorhythms. There are also educational, game, and graphics programs. *32 BASIC Programs for the Apple Computer* is sold as a book/software package.
dilithium Press; 16K, one disk drive; book, $19.95, book and software package, $39.95.

Games

If you use the Apple as a serious tool in business and at home, you'll probably become so efficient that you'll have lots of spare time on your hands. The Apple can help with that, too. Many excellent entertainment games exist to help you while away the hours. Most of them are not only fun, but also help sharpen problem-solving skills, or promote eye-hand coordination.

Sargon II. Sargon is the computer chess champion. Whether you are a beginner or a chess expert, Sargon's seven levels of difficulty can match your skill level. The chessboard is displayed in high-resolution graphics as you play. With the "kibitz" option, Sargon will even give you a hint — or set a trap for you.
Hayden Book Company; 48K, one disk drive; $35.

Telengard. Descend into a 50-level dungeon where horrible monsters lurk in search of treasure and power. Players choose the character attributes such as weapons, intelligence, strength, and experience before the journey. The program demands quick decision-making, because the game is played in real time. It can be addictive.
Avalon Hill Company; 48K, one disk drive; $28.

Seafox. Command a lone submarine on your high-resolution screen and pursue the convoy of enemy ships. If you can avoid menacing mines,

Moon Patrol. This is a fast, furious game for one or two players. Land your spacecraft on the lunar surface while dodging and shooting alien invaders. The graphic presentation is striking and rivals many arcade games. Four levels of difficulty are incorporated into the game.
Avalon Hill Company; 48K, one disk drive; $25.

Road to Gettysburg. Could you have won the battle of Gettysburg? Find out with this game, which recreates the feel of command of an American Civil War army. You have to contend with a frustrating dispatch system that the actual generals used in 1863. Players also must deal with possible misinterpretation of orders, troop fatigue, or even disobedience — just as the real commanders did. Two scenarios are available, both based on historical facts. Play against another player or let the computer control the opposing force.
Strategic Simulations; 48K, one disk drive; $60.

Arcade Machine. Most of us have played arcade games, but this program lets you create your own! No knowledge of programming is necessary. Games will have such features as animated full-color monsters and other players selected or designed by you. Dramatic shoot-em-up explosions and sound effects can be included. Various levels of difficulty and the number of players may be built into your customized game. A colorful title with your name will appear on the screen as the program is **RUN**.
Broderbund Software; 48K, one disk drive; $45.

UTILITY PROGRAMS — AIDS FOR THE PROGRAMMER

Utility programs help you get the most from your equipment and software. If you write your own programs, many utility programs can enhance your programs and make your programming more efficient.

The Graphics Magician. This program lets you create smooth animation to include in your own programs. Create hundreds of high-resolution pictures in more than 100 colors, and save them on disk. Instructions on how to include these in your programs are provided.
Penguin Software; 48K, one disk drive; $60.

Apple-Cillin II. This is a comprehensive diagnostic system developed to check the performance of your Apple and its accessories. It will verify more than two dozen hardware operations ranging from the CPU operation to disk drive speed and either identify a specific problem or give your computer system a clean bill of health. Results of the test may be printed on your printer. Available for IIe only.
XPS Software; 48K, one disk drive; $50.

Printer Control Program (PCP). PCP allows owners to set up their Epson MX-80 printer to print boldface, compressed characters, variable line spacing, slashed zeros, and elongated characters. Instructions are provided so these features can be included in BASIC programs or in the Applewriter word processor or Visicalc programs.

Pro/Pac; 32K, one disk drive, printer; $25.

DOS Tool Kit. The DOS Tool Kit is a collection of programs and subroutines designed to aid the Applesoft programmer. It gives the programmer the ability to easily perform such functions as renumbering programs, merging programs, deleting remarks from BASIC programs, and searching for strings or variables. Also included are two programs which help the user create high-resolution characters and two graphics demonstration programs.

Apple Computer; 48K, one disk drive; $50.

Copy II +. This program provides the user with the ability to make backup copies of protected software — that is, programs designed to prevent copying. While many copy-protected programs can be copied with this program, some are difficult to copy and require a trial-and-error process. A list of popular commercial programs and the instructions necessary to copy them comes with the program.

Central Point Software; 48K, two disk drives; $50.

Summing Up

The programs listed here are but a sampling of the vast amount of software available for the Apple. More programs are coming on the market every day. You'll learn where to find out about many additional programs in Chapter 8.

PRODUCERS OF COMPUTER SOFTWARE DISCUSSED IN CHAPTER 7

Avalon-Hill Game Company, 4517 Harford Rd., Baltimore, MD 21214. (Moon Patrol, Telengard)

Broderbund Software, 1938 Fourth St., San Rafael, CA 94901. (Seafox, Arcade Machine, Bank Street Writer)

dilithium Press, 8285 S.W. Nimbus, Suite 151, Beaverton, OR 97005. (*32 BASIC Programs for the Apple Computer*)

Virtual Combinatics, 35 Main St., Rockport, MA 01966. (Micro Cookbook, Micro Barmate)

User Friendly Systems, 6135 Ross Rd., Fairfield, OH 45014. (The Genealogist's Right Hand)

Lightning Software, Box 1725, Palo Alto, CA 94360. (Master Type)

Pro/Pac, 14925 Memorial Dr., Suite 105, Houston, TX 77079. (Printer Control Program (PCP))

Sensible Software, 6619 Perham Dr., West Bloomfield, MI 48033. (Sensible Speller IV)

Kensington Microware, 919 Third Ave., New York, NY 10022. (Format II)

Individualized Operand, Box 3030, San Rafael, CA 94912. (Accurec)

Stoneware, 50 Belvedere St., San Rafael, CA 94901. (DB Master III)

Osborne/McGraw-Hill, 630 Bancroft Way, Berkeley, CA 94710. (Micro-Finesse)

Continental Software, 16724 Hawthorne Blvd., Lawndale, CA 90260. (The Home Accountant)

Strategic Simulations, 465 Fairchild Dr., Suite 108, Mountain View, CA 94043. (The Road to Gettysburg)

Penguin Software, 830 4th Ave., Geneva, IL 60134. (The Graphics Magician)

XPS Software, 323 York Rd., Carlisle, PA 17013. (Apple-Cillin)

Apple Computer Corporation, 20525 Mariani Ave., Cupertino, CA 95014. (Supermath, LOGO, Don't Fall, Datatree, DOS Tool Kit)

Sunbelt Computing, 7807 Kenosha, Lubbock, TX 79423. (Spelling Tutor, Teacher's Helper)

Synergistic Software, 5221 120th St. S.W., Bellevue WA 98006. (The Inventory Manager, Mailing List Database)

BPI Systems, 3423 Guadalupe, Austin, TX 78705. (BPI General Ledger Accounting, BPI Job Cost)

Central Point Software, Box 19730, Portland, OR 97219. (Copy II+)

Mesa Research, Rt. 1, Box 1456A, Waco, TX 76710. (Investment Decisions)

SFA Enterprises, Box 33511, Northglenn, CO 80233. (Household Inventory Program)

Hayden Book Co., 50 Essex St., Rochelle Park, NJ 07662. (Sargon II)

Micro Program Designs, 5440 Crestline Rd., Wilmington, DE 19808. (Stock Market Tycoon)

Sof/Sys, 4306 Upton Ave. S., Minneapolis, MN 55410. (Executive Secretary)

Sterling Swift Publishing Co., 1600 Fortview Rd., Austin, TX 78704. (How to Program in the B.A.S.I.C.)

Educational Activities, Box 392, Freeport, NY 11520. (Spelltronics)

Orange Cherry Media, 7 Delano Dr., Bedford Hills, NY 10507. (Adventures around the World)

J & S Software, 140 Reide Ave., Port Washington, NY 11050. (Apple Gradebook)

Ideatech Co., Box 62451, Sunnyvale, CA 94088. (Basic Electricity)

Micro Learningware, Box 2134, N. Mankato, MN 56001. (History and Geography Package)

Micro Power and Light, 12820 Hillcrest Rd., Suite 224, Dallas, TX 75230. (Library Skills)

Minnesota Educational Computing Consortium (MECC), 2520 Broadway Dr., St. Paul, MN 55113. (Oregon)

Computer Using Educators (CUE), 333 Main St., Redwood City, CA 94063. (Multiplication Bingo)

VisiCorp, 1330 Bordeaux Dr., Sunnyvale, CA 94086. (VisiCalc)

Chapter 8

Sources of Additional Information

This has been a good beginning for anyone interested in serious use of the Apple. Yet there is much more to be learned about the Apple computer and personal computing. We want to provide you with some clues about how to get the additional information you need.

MAGAZINES

Several magazines are published just for Apple users. General computing magazines also are useful sources of information for Apple users. Teachers and other educators will be interested in educational computing journals. Brief reviews of the best of these follow. Because subscription rates are subject to change, you may want to contact the publisher for current rates before you subscribe.

Magazines for Apple Users Only

Apple Orchard
908 George St.
Santa Clara, CA 95050
Subscription: $19.50/9 issues
Apple Orchard is published by the International Apple Core (IAC). The magazine features articles, program listings, news from Apple clubs, software and new product reviews, and advertisements.

Nibble
Box 325
Lincoln, MA 01773
Subscription: $19.50/8 issues
This magazine contains program listings, tips for Apple users, and software reviews. Most programs are oriented either toward business/finance or games. Programs published in *Nibble* may be typed into the

computer by the user from the listings in the magazine and saved on disk or they may be ordered on disk from *Nibble* for about $20 each. *Nibble* is a good source of inexpensive software.

Call-A.P.P.L.E.
Apple Puget Sound Program Library Exchange
304 Main Ave. S., Suite 300
Renton, WA 98055
Subscription: $40/8 issues

This monthly magazine is the publication of the world's largest group of Apple computer users. The group also maintains a hotline to answer member questions about products for the Apple and programming problems. Special publications and software are also available. The magazine is an excellent source of programming tips. It also contains hardware and software reviews and program listings. Much of the material assumes programming experience, but the hotline can save beginners and experienced users alike much frustration.

Peelings
2260 Oleander St.
Las Cruces, NM 88004
Subscription: $21/9 issues

This is a collection of Apple software reviews. The reviews are thorough and don't mince words. If a program is a lemon, this publication will tell you that it is. It also provides information on the capabilities of the software that others miss.

Apple Magazine
1260 Bandley Dr.
Cupertino, CA 95050
Subscription: Occasional/free

This is the Apple Computer Corporation's quarterly catalog disguised as a magazine. It contains several short articles and provides an up-to-date listing of all hardware and software marketed by the company. It is available from Apple dealers and is usually given free to customers.

Hardcore Computing
Dept. 33
14404 East D St.
Tacoma, WA 98445
Subscription: $20/6 issues

This is a controversial magazine. Some publications refuse to carry its ads because it promotes unauthorized copying of copyrighted programs.

Hardcore advertises that it will show you how to "backup any diskette . . . do and undo copy-protection . . . and customize commercial programs." It also includes articles, program tricks, software reviews, and program listings.

General-Interest Computer Magazines

Creative Computing
Box 789-M
Morrison, NJ 07960
Subscription: $25/12 issues
  If you plan to subscribe to only one computer magazine, this would be a good choice. *Creative Computing* has all types of articles, reviews, program listings, and departments as well as a sense of humor. It is sprinkled with cartoons, satire, short stories, puzzles, and even an occasional poem. Lots of advertisements for discount hardware and software are included.

BYTE
Box 590
Martinsville, NJ 08836
Subscription: $19/12 issues
  BYTE is a highly technical magazine that will bewilder the beginning Apple user. *BYTE* will appeal to computer hobbyists who have their basements crammed with gadgets and like to experiment. About the only feature the rest of us will enjoy are the remarkable covers that will undoubtedly become classics. *BYTE* does publish many detailed, informative articles if you want in-depth presentations on a topic.

Microcomputing
Box 977
Farmingdale, NY 11737
Subscription: $25/12 issues
  Microcomputing is a comprehensive, carefully edited publication noted for excellent articles on technical topics and for regular features on the microcomputer industry, education, business, and new products and publications. Advanced computer users may prefer it to *Creative Computing*.

Popular Computing
70 Main St.
Peterborough, NH 03458
Subscription: $15/12 issues
  PC is aimed at new microcomputer owners and browsers. It contains easy-to-read reviews and articles on microcomputers, accessories, software,

and new products — all of which are well illustrated. It is an excellent magazine for beginners.

Softalk
11021 Magnolia Blvd.
North Hollywood, CA 91601
Subscription: $24/12 issues

Softalk features chatty articles on the people in the microcomputer industry, a reader's forum, a programming contest page, and a list of best-selling programs for the Apple.

Softside
Box 68
Milford, NH 03055
Subscription: $24/12 issues

This magazine is devoted largely to printed games software for the Apple, PET, TRS-80, Atari, and IBM PC computers. It also has tips for programmers. It is a good source of inexpensive software.

Magazines for Educators

Apple Education News
Bos 20485
San Jose, CA 95106
Subscription: Occasional/free

This newsletter is published occasionally by Apple Computer Corporation. It is a good source of information on CAI software published by schools, colleges, and commercial publishers. It also contains glowing accounts of the company's products. The newsletter is distributed free through computer stores.

Classroom Computer Learning
Box 266
Cambridge, MA 02139
Subscription: $16/10 issues

CCL is a good source of software reviews and easy-to-understand articles on school use of computers. News items such as conference announcements, new products, and pending legislation also are included.

The Computing Teacher
Eastern Oregon State College
La Grande, OR 97850
Subscription: $20/9 issues

This journal features articles on teacher education, computer-based instruction, and the impact of computers on the curriculum. The journal focuses on practical ideas for the use of computers in the public school curriculum.

Educational Computer Magazine
Box 535
Cupertino, CA 95015
Subscription: $15/10 issues

EC contains information on educational computing at all levels. Easy-to-read articles, software reviews, new product announcements, and new items are featured. Regular departments include computers in the media center, free and inexpensive software reviews, and advice to computer users.

Electronic Learning
Scholastic Inc.
Box 2001
Englewood Cliffs, NJ 07632
Subscription: $18/8 issues

Electronic Learning is colorful and easy to read. Recent issues have contained articles on computer literacy, a microcomputer purchasing guide and a tutorial of software evaluation. Teachers will find this journal a good source of ideas for classroom projects.

Educational Technology
140 Sylvan Ave.
Englewood Cliffs, NJ 07632
Subscription: $49/12 issues

This is a monthly publication for educational technologists and audiovisual specialists. It contains mostly research papers written in academic language. The journal has concentrated on computer uses in education in recent years but it is not limited to that topic. It is a good source of footnotes for term papers.

Technological Horizons in Education (T.H.E. Journal)
Box 992
Action, MD 21072
Subscription: Free/12 issues

T.H.E. Journal contains short reviews on new equipment and software, short articles on theoretical and practical aspects of technological advances in education, and lots of advertising. Subscriptions are free to school administrators.

APPLE USER GROUPS

These user groups are clubs for Apple users. Most major U.S. cities have Apple User Groups that are affiliated with the International Apple Core (IAC). The IAC publication, *Apple Orchard,* was described earlier. Most clubs meet once a month to discuss topics of common concern to Apple users, to listen to presentations related to Apple use, and to swap software. Each user group is sent public domain disks from IAC on a regular basis. These may be copied freely by members. Most user groups have their own newsletter. Some clubs sponsor computer fairs, electronic bulletin boards, and other services for members. Some clubs sponsor cooperative purchasing of blank disks, software, and equipment to give members the best prices. Membership fees are usually minimal. We have found Apple user groups to be very worthwhile — mainly because of the free software and the ideas gained from chatting with other Apple users.

Because officers of local clubs change often, they will not be listed here. You can get information on the Apple Users Group nearest you from most Apple dealers, by contacting the IAC, or from the regional IAC coordinators listed.

International Apple Core
908 George St.
Santa Clara, CA 95050
408-727-7652

IAC Regional Directors:

Region	Area covered	Regional Director	Telephone
1	CA zips 94100 and up WA, OR, NV, HI, AK and Am Samoa	Stephen Lloyd	415-571-7370
2	CA zips 94009 and lower	Jim Simpson	805-492-3391
3	AZ, NM, TX, OK, AR, MO, LA, MS, TN	Mike Kramer	215-356-6183
4	ID, UT, MT, WY, CO, ND, SD, NE, KS, MN, IA	Bob Sader-Cederlof	214-324-2050
5	WI, IL, MI, IN, KY	Barry Bayer	312-798-6496
6	PA, NJ, FL	Neil Lipson	215-356-6183
7	ME, CT, MA, NH, RI, VT, NY, DC	Robert Ramsdell	617-546-3104
8	OH, WV, MD, DE, VA, NC, SC, GA, AL	Tom Wysocki	216-942-7086

BOOKS AND BOOK PUBLISHERS

A stroll through either your local Apple dealer's book section or a general bookstore is likely to show you just how popular the Apple really is. There are at least 100 different books that are either specifically about the Apple computer or are directly related to its use. Most bookstores will have only a few of these. Apple dealers are likely to have some titles too. This section will not include all Apple-related books currently on the market. There are just too many, and new books are appearing regularly. Instead, some of the more popular publishers will be noted and a representative sample of their publications will be described.

dilithium Press
Box 606
Beaverton, OR 97075
800-547-1842

Dilithium is the publisher of this book as well as more than 100 other books on personal computing. Most of them are on a beginning or intermediate level. You can get a free catalog by writing or phoning the toll-free number given above.

One dilithium publication is: *32 BASIC Programs for the Apple Computer.* This book sells for $19.95. As the title implies, it is a book of programs for the Apple. It includes games, simple business programs, and programs for home use. The programs are explained and listed in the book. They may be typed in from the listing in the book or they may be ordered on disk for another $19.95. All programs are guaranteed to work.

Another dililthium publication which is one of our favorites is: *How to Make Money with Your Microcomputer*, which gave us the idea for writing this book. It covers writing for publication, conducting workshops and seminars, proposal writing, software publishing, and operating a computer store. The 154-page book sells for $13.95.

Brooks/Cole Publishing Co.
Belmont, CA 94002

Brooks/Cole is a division of Wadsworth of Belmont, California. They publish about a dozen books on computer science and computer education. Most are on the intermediate or advanced levels. Their titles include: *BASIC: An Introduction to Computer Programming with the Apple,* and

An Apple for the Teacher. The first title is one of many titles on programming the Apple in Applesoft BASIC. *An Apple for the Teacher* is a delightful book for teachers. It covers computer programming and instructional design of computer-assisted instruction materials.

Creative Computing Press
Morris Plains, NJ 07950
800-631-8112

The publisher of *Creative Computing* magazine brings us several useful books on personal computing. A free catalog may be ordered by writing or calling the toll-free number. One of the most popular titles is *Katie and the Computer*. This is a delightful picture/adventure book that explains how a computer works to children from 4 to 10. The 42-page book is $6.95.

BYTE Books
70 Main St.
Peterborough, NH 03458
800-258-5420

The publisher of *BYTE* magazine produces several books on the intermediate and advanced levels. One of their best is *Apple Logo* which is a unique guide to the applications of the Logo language. The author introduces programming techniques, turtle graphics, and geometric concepts. The book also includes a reference manual of enduring value to sophisticated Logo users. The 240-page book is $14.95. This book, as well as the catalog, may be requested by writing or phoning the toll-free number.

McGraw-Hill Book Co.
1221 Avenue of the Americas
New York, NY 03458

One of the largest publishers in the world, McGraw-Hill, has recently attempted to cash in on the market in personal computing. *Apple Pascal: A Hands-On Approach* provides 14 hands-on tutorials to provide a working knowledge of the Pascal programming language. The $14.95 book is appropriate for either classroom or self-study.

Apple Computer Corporation
20525 Mariani Ave.
Cupertino, CA 95014
408-996-1010

The Apple Computer Corporation publishes several manuals that are sold through Apple dealers. However, these are overpriced and incomplete. The most important of these for Apple IIe, II+, and II owners are reviewed only because they are in such widespread use:

The Applesoft BASIC Programming Reference Manual (for Apple IIe only). This manual was referred to in Chapter 5 of this book. The latest version comes in a three-volume set which costs about $40. It can be purchased in most computer stores. The manual is well done, but it leaves out some important things and is overpriced. We feel that your money would be better spent on one of the independently published programming manuals. This manual is for IIe users only and should not be purchased by II+ and II users.

The Apple II DOS Manual. This manual usually is supplied with the disk II interface card when it is purchased. It also can be purchased separately for about $10. It explains use of the Apple's D.O.S. 3.3 operating system and use of the Disk II drive. It is companion manual to the *Programming Reference Manual* and is a necessity for serious programmers who use Apple's programming manual noted earlier. It is appropriate for IIe, II+, or II users.

The BASIC Programming Reference Manual is a pre-IIe publication in one volume that sells for about $10. It is designed for II+ and II users but it can also be used by IIe users.

Other Books for Apple Users

Programming the Apple
Mesa Research
Rt. 1
Waco, TX 76710

This book is an excellent and thorough programming manual for those seriously interested in learning Applesoft BASIC. It also includes many sample programs, including a set of useful, sophisticated programs called Financial Decisions. The 534-page book sells for about $17 and may be ordered by mail or purchased in many computer stores. It is a good alternative to the *Applesoft BASIC Programming Reference Manual* published by Apple Computer.

COMPUTER SHOWS AND CONFERENCES

Each year there are many exhibits, trade shows, and professional conferences that deal with personal computers in business, education, and personal use. It would be impossible to list all of these, but the largest and those of greatest interest to Apple users are noted here. These meetings are fascinating. They also are an excellent way to see all the new products first-hand and to listen to presentations on innovative applications of personal computers.

AppleFests

Northeast Expositions Inc. sponsors the annual AppleFest computer shows. Two of these are held currently — one on the East coast and one on the West. The specific locations of these will vary yearly. The AppleFests are the world's largest expositions exclusively for Apple owners. The shows feature hundreds of exhibits of the newest products for the Apple. Every conceivable application is covered — from arcade games to accounting packages. All products are for sale at special show prices. Seminars, tutorials, and workshops are included on the three-day program. Tickets are $10 for one day (exhibits only) or $25 for the entire three-day conference and exhibits. AppleFests usually are held in the fall of the year. Announcements on AppleFests will be carried in *Apple Orchard* magazine and most other computer magazines, or you can call Northeast Expositions toll-free at 800-841-7000.

Computer Trade Shows

Computer shows are held from time to time in most major cities across the United States. The shows provide computer hardware and software vendors the opportunity to show their wares to the public. Trade shows include Apple products as well as those for other computers. Hundreds of exhibits are likely to be present. These shows are an excellent place to see the new products and buy them at discount prices. Product demonstrations will be included, but most shows do not include seminars or workshops. For current information on local computer shows in your area, watch your local newspaper or the computer magazines discussed earlier. National and international shows usually are announced in the computer magazines.

The National Computing Conference (NCC). This is the largest and oldest computing conference. It is held in a different city each year. In 1983, the conference drew more than 100,000 participants. All types of computers, software, and products are in the huge exhibit display that includes at least 3,200 exhibitors. Experts from various fields present sessions on almost every aspect of computing during the four-day conference. The conference is held in the spring of each year. Watch the computer magazines for announcements.

National Educational Computing Conference (NECC). NECC is the educational cousin of NCC. Like NCC, the annual conference is rotated to different regions of the country each year. It is the largest national conference for educators at all levels. It includes exhibits as well as seminars, workshops, and forums. NECC is held in the early summer of each year. Educators interested in attending should watch any of the educational computing magazines noted earlier for announncements.

SOME FINAL WORDS

We hope you have found this book useful and that you continue to explore the world of personal computing. If you have any suggestions you feel would improve the next edition of this book, please write to us in care of dilithium Press. Happy computing!

Appendix C

Applesoft Legal Variable Names

	A	B	C	D	E	F	G	H	I	J	K	L	M	N	O	P	Q	R
A = A	AA	AB	AC	AD	AE	AF	AG	AH	AI	AJ	AK	AL	AM	AN	AO	AP	AQ	AR
B = B	BA	BB	BC	BD	BE	BF	BG	BH	BI	BJ	BK	BL	BM	BN	BO	BP	BQ	BR
C = C	CA	CB	CC	CD	CE	CF	CG	CH	CI	CJ	CK	CL	CM	CN	CO	CP	CQ	CR
D = D	DA	DB	DC	DD	DE	DF	DG	DH	DI	DJ	DK	DL	DM	DN	DO	DP	DQ	DR
E = E	EA	EB	EC	ED	EE	EF	EG	EH	EI	EJ	EK	EL	EM	EN	EO	EP	EQ	ER
F = F	FA	FB	FC	FD	FE	FF	FG	FH	FI	FJ	FK	FL	FM		FO	FP	FQ	FR
G = G	GA	GB	GC	GD	GE	GF	GG	GH	GI	GJ	GK	GL	GM	GN		GP	GQ	
H = H	HA	HB	HC	HD	HE	HF	HG	HH	HI	HJ	HK	HL	HM	HN	HO	HP	HQ	HR
I = I	IA	IB	IC	ID	IE		IG	IH	II	IJ	IK	IL	IM		IO	IP	IQ	IR
J = J	JA	JB	JC	JD	JE	JF	JG	JH	JI	JJ	JK	JL	JM	JN	JO	JP	JQ	JR
K = K	KA	KB	KC	KD	KE	KF	KG	KH	KI	KJ	KK	KL	KM	KN	KO	KP	KQ	KR
L = L	LA	LB	LC	LD	LE	LF	LG	LH	LI	LJ	LK	LL	LM	LN	LO	LP	LQ	LR
M = M	MA	MB	MC	MD	ME	MF	MG	MH	MI	MJ	MK	ML	MM	MN	MO	MP	MQ	MR
N = N	NA	NB	NC	ND	NE	NF	NG	NH	NI	NJ	NK	NL	NM	NN	NO	NP	NQ	NR
O = O	OA	OB	OC	OD	OE	OF	OG	OH	OI	OJ	OK	OL	OM		OO	OP	OQ	
P = P	PA	PB	PC	PD	PE	PF	PG	PH	PI	PJ	PK	PL	PM	PN	PO	PP	PQ	
Q = Q	QA	QB	QC	QD	QE	QF	QG	QH	QI	QJ	QK	QL	QM	QN	QO	QP	QQ	QR
R = R	RA	RB	RC	RD	RE	RF	RG	RH	RI	RJ	RK	RL	RM	RN	RO	RP	RQ	RR
S = S	SA	SB	SC	SD	SE	SF	SG	SH	SI	SJ	SK	SL	SM	SN	SO	SP	SQ	SR
T = T	TA	TB	TC	TD	TE	TF	TG	TH	TI	TJ	TK	TL	TM	TN		TP	TQ	TR
U = U	UA	UB	UC	UD	UE	UF	UG	UH	UI	UJ	UK	UL	UM	UN	UO	UP	UQ	UR
V = V	VA	VB	VC	VD	VE	VF	VG	VH	VI	VJ	VK	VL	VM	VN	VO	VP	VQ	VR
W = W	WA	WB	WC	WD	WE	WF	WG	WH	WI	WJ	WK	WL	WM	WN	WO	WP	WQ	WR
X = X	XA	XB	XC	XD	XE	XF	XG	XH	XI	XJ	XK	XL	XM	XN	XO	XP	XQ	XR
Y = Y	YA	YB	YC	YD	YE	YF	YG	YH	YI	YJ	YK	YL	YM	YN	YO	YP	YQ	YR
Z = Z	ZA	ZB	ZC	ZD	ZE	ZF	ZG	ZH	ZI	ZJ	ZK	ZL	ZM	ZN	ZO	ZP	ZQ	ZR

Notes:
*Use separate tables for numeric and string variables.
*Blank filled variables are illegal.

	S	T	U	V	W	X	Y	Z	0	1	2	3	4	5	6	7	8	9
AS		AU	AV	AW	AX	AY	AZ	A0	A1	A2	A3	A4	A5	A6	A7	A8	A9
BS	BT	BU	BV	BW	BX	BY	BZ	B0	B1	B2	B3	B4	B5	B6	B7	B8	B9
CS	CT	CU	CV	CW	CX	CY	CZ	C0	C1	C2	C3	C4	C5	C6	C7	C8	C9
DS	DT	DU	DV	DW	DX	DY	DZ	D0	D1	D2	D3	D4	D5	D6	D7	D8	D9
ES	ET	EU	EV	EW	EX	EY	EZ	E0	E1	E2	E3	E4	E5	E6	E7	E8	E9
FS	FT	FU	FV	FW	FX	FY	FZ	F0	F1	F2	F3	F4	F5	F6	F7	F8	F9
GS	GT	GU	GV	GW	GX	GY	GZ	G0	G1	G2	G3	G4	G5	G6	G7	G8	G9
HS	HT	HU	HV	HW	HX	HY	HZ	H0	H1	H2	H3	H4	H5	H6	H7	H8	H9
IS	IT	IU	IV	IW	IX	IY	IZ	I0	I1	I2	I3	I4	I5	I6	I7	I8	I9
JS	JT	JU	JV	JW	JX	JY	JZ	J0	J1	J2	J3	J4	J5	J6	J7	J8	J9
KS	KT	KU	KV	KW	KX	KY	KZ	K0	K1	K2	K3	K4	K5	K6	K7	K8	K9
LS	LT	LU	LV	LW	LX	LY	LZ	L0	L1	L2	L3	L4	L5	L6	L7	L8	L9
MS	MT	MU	MV	MW	MX	MY	MZ	M0	M1	M2	M3	M4	M5	M6	M7	M8	M9
NS	NT	NU	NV	NW	NX	NY	NZ	N0	N1	N2	N3	N4	N5	N6	N7	N8	N9
OS	OT	OU	OV	OW	OX	OY	OZ	O0	O1	O2	O3	O4	O5	O6	O7	O8	O9
PS	PT	PU	PV	PW	PX	PY	PZ	P0	P1	P2	P3	P4	P5	P6	P7	P8	P9
QS	QT	QU	QV	QW	QX	QY	QZ	Q0	Q1	Q2	Q3	Q4	Q5	Q6	Q7	Q8	Q9
RS	RT	RU	RV	RW	RX	RY	RZ	R0	R1	R2	R3	R4	R5	R6	R7	R8	R9
SS	ST	SU	SV	SW	SX	SY	SZ	S0	S1	S2	S3	S4	S5	S6	S7	S8	S9
TS	TT	TU	TV	TW	TX	TY	TZ	T0	T1	T2	T3	T4	T5	T6	T7	T8	T9
US	UT	UU	UV	UW	UX	UY	UZ	U0	U1	U2	U3	U4	U5	U6	U7	U8	U9
VS	VT	VU	VV	VW	VX	VY	VZ	V0	V1	V2	V3	V4	V5	V6	V7	V8	V9
WS	WT	WU	WV	WW	WX	WY	WZ	W0	W1	W2	W3	W4	W5	W6	W7	W8	W9
XS	XT	XU	XV	XW	XX	XY	XZ	X0	X1	X2	X3	X4	X5	X6	X7	X8	X9
YS	YT	YU	YV	YW	YX	YY	YZ	Y0	Y1	Y2	Y3	Y4	Y5	Y6	Y7	Y8	Y9
ZS	ZT	ZU	ZV	ZW	ZX	ZY	ZZ	Z0	Z1	Z2	Z3	Z4	Z5	Z6	Z7	Z8	Z9

Trademark
Acknowledgements

Acc Rec
Adam and Eve
Advanced Logic Systems
Adventures Around the World
Amdek
Apple
Apple Cat II
Apple Computer, Inc.
Apple Grade Book
Apple II
Apple II +
Apple IIe
Apple III
Apple-Cillin III
Applesoft BASIC
Appletalker
Appletime Clock
Arcade Machine
Atari
Avalon Hill Co.
Bank Street Writer
Basic Electricity
BPI General Leger Accounting
BPI Job Cost
Broderbund Software
Central Point Software
Chevrolet
Com-Star f/t
CompuServe

Computers International
Continental Software
Cool-Mark II
Copy II +
CUE
Daisywriter 2000
Dan Palmer LCA-1
Dan Palmer LCA-2
Datatree
DB Master III
Don't Ask Software
Don't Fall
DOS Tool Kit
Echo GP
Electronics Protection Devices
Epson FX-80
Epson RX-80
Executive Secretary
Format II
Graphics Magician
Guardian Angel
Hayden Book Co.
History and Geography Package
Household Inventory
How to Program in BASIC
Ideatech Co.
Individualized Operand
Inventory Manager
Investment Decisions

Jade
JDR Microdevices
J&S Software
Kensington Microware
Krell Logo
Lemon Surge Protector
Library Skills
Lightning Software
Lisa
Lobo Drives International
Macintosh
Mailing List Data Base
Mark Four Imports
Master Type
MBI Corp.
Mega Research
Micro Barmate
Micro Cookbook
Micro Finesse
Micro Learningware
Micro Power and Light Co.
Micro Program Designs
Micro Users Software Exchange
Micro-Sci
Microsoft
Minnesota Educational Computing
  Consortium
Moon Patrol
Mountain Computer
Multiplication Bingo
NEC
Novation
Okidata 2350
Okidata ML/92
Orange Cherry Media
Oregon
Osborne/McGraw-Hill
Penguin Software
Printer Control Program
Pro/Pac
Protecto Enterprises
R/H Electronics

Radio Shack
Rixon PC 300
Road to Gettysburg
SAM Speech Synthesizer
Sargon II
Saturn
Seafox
Sensible Software
Sensible Speller IV
SFA Enterprises
Silentype II
Smith Corona TP-2
Sof/Sys
Software Automatic Mouth
Software Co.
Space Invaders
SSM Apple Modemcard
Sterling Swift Publishing Co.
Stock Market Tycoon
Stoneware
Strategic Simulations
Street Electronics
Sunbelt Computing
SuperCalc
Superfan II
Supermath
Synergistic Software
System Saver
Telengard
The Geneologist's Right Hand
The Home Accountant
The Source
Thunderclock Plus
Thunderware Products
TRS-80
User Friendly Systems
Viewmax-80
Virtual Comginatics
VisiCalc
VisiCorp
VOICE
West Side Electronics

WordStar
XPS Software
Z-Card
Zenith

Index